"Fastnet, Force **10**"

70N·020W 4541

60N·020W 1539

50N·010W 1535

# "Fastnet, Force 10"

## John Rousmaniere

W · W · NORTON & COMPANY

NEW YORK · LONDON

PRECEDING PHOTOGRAPHS A satellite photograph of the eastern North Atlantic Ocean, taken on August 13, 1979. *U.S. National Oceanographic and Atmospheric Administration.* Fastnet Rock, Tuesday, August 14. *Irish Times.*

---

THE TEXT of this book is composed in photocomposition Caledonia, with display type set in Eurostile. Composition and manufacturing are by the Maple Vail Book Manufacturing Group. Maps by Peter Milne. Drawings by Richard Everitt. Book design by Marjorie J. Flock.

*First Edition*

Library of Congress Cataloging in Publication Data
Rousmaniere, John.
    "Fastnet, Force 10."
    Bibliography: p.
    Includes index.
    1. Fastnet Yacht Race.   I. Title.
GV832.R68   1980       797.1'4      80–12760

ISBN 0 393–03256–6

1 2 3 4 5 6 7 8 9 0

For Will and Dana

# Contents

# Maps

# Foreword

**T**HIS IS A SEA STORY, and it is true. It is the story of how fifteen people died, not in wartime, or on a hunt for whales, or in a typhoon in the South China Sea, but during a yacht race only seventy miles off the coast of England. What began as a six hundred-mile sail in fine weather around a lighthouse off the Irish coast became, for twenty-seven hundred men and women in 303 yachts, a terrifying ordeal as one of the most vicious summer gales in the twentieth century swept east from the American Great Plains to trap the Fastnet race fleet in the shallow waters of the Western Approaches to Britain.

The worst disaster in the one-hundred year history of ocean yacht racing, the 1979 Fastnet race is a startling reminder of man's vulnerability before the elements. As the official inquiry into the calamity concluded, "the sea showed that it can be a deadly enemy and that those who go to sea for pleasure must do so in the full knowledge that they may encounter dangers of the highest order." From 10:00 P.M. on August 13 until 6:00 P.M. on August 14, those dangers were a shrieking wind that blew at force 10 velocity (forty-eight to fifty-five knots) and up to hurricane strength, and, more dangerous, a true maelstrom of a seaway. Steep waves as high as fifty feet formed towering breakers that collapsed on boats and sailors like surf on a beach, hurling twenty thousand pounds of water at twenty or thirty knots onto hulls that, on average, were only thirty-eight feet long and weighed about fifteen thousand pounds. More than one-third of the boats were knocked over until their masts paralleled the water. One-fourth were capsized entirely, many rolling over through a circle. Even the larger boats—among them former prime minister Edward Heath's *Morning Cloud* and Ted Turner's *Tenacious*—were battered. Many boats were damaged and some crews were badly injured.

Worse yet, six men were lost overboard and swept away

when their safety harnesses broke. Nine others drowned or died of hypothermia in the cold water and air, either on board yachts or near life rafts that had capsized. In all, twenty-four crews abandoned their yachts, five of which sank. One hundred and thirty-six men and women were saved from sinking yachts, life rafts, and the water itself by heroic helicopter crews, commercial and naval seamen, and fellow yachtsmen, and seventy yachtsmen were towed or escorted to safety by lifeboats.

What follows is the story of the race and the storm, told in the accounts of over seventy yachts and rescue vessels.

"This is the disintegrating power of a great wind: it isolates one from one's kind," Joseph Conrad wrote in *Typhoon*. Besides affection for the outdoors and competitiveness, one of the reasons why people undergo the rigors of racing boats out of sight of land is the opportunity that the sport offers for companionship. The Fastnet gale, however, showed how isolated and helpless we all can be. Human contact was difficult and communication was impossible in the shrieking wind and pounding seas. Even the security of the cabins was false, as galley stoves, tins of food, sails, and bodies flew from side to side below with every lurch and roll. While offshore sailing had always been respected as a challenge and, at worst, a risk, few people caught in the gale would have previously thought the sport to be actually dangerous. The realization that they, their shipmates, and their competitors were in danger dawned on the most unlucky sailors during the gale, and on many of the survivors after the storm passed and the fight for survival ended.

Acknowledging vulnerability has not driven this sailor from the sea. I had seen gales before the Fastnet race—but none as bad—and probably will see gales again—I hope, none worse. Yet like many people at the turn of the decade, I feel considerably more aware of the limitations both of myself and of the increasingly complex technology that surrounds my sport and my life. Like many activities in late twentieth-century life, yachting apparently has benefited from professionalism, specialization, and rationality. In the year of a famine in Southeast Asia, a revolution in Iran, and a frightening accident at a nuclear power plant in Pennsylvania, the calamity in the Western Approaches seems to be yet another indication that our positivistic faith in technology may be groundless. We appear to have been led by transitory successes into the heresy that we can completely manipulate our lives and our environments—a modern version of the medieval doctrine of justification by works.

Hunger, religious fervor, and nuclear energy may eventually be channeled or controlled, but only with the deepest respect for their latent powers. More certainly, wind and water will again be used for emotionally satisfying ends, but only by people who acknowledge that catastrophe is always possible.

John Rousmaniere

*Stamford, Connecticut*
*December 26, 1979*

FORCE 10: Wind speed, forty-eight to fifty-five knots. Very high waves with long overhanging crests. The resulting foam in great patches is blown in dense white streaks along the direction of the wind. On the whole the surface of the sea takes a white appearance. The tumbling of the sea becomes heavy and shocklike. Visibility affected.

— Beaufort scale of wind and sea conditions

BOATSWAIN: *What cares these roarers for the name of king? To cabin! Silence! Trouble us not!*

— William Shakespeare, *The Tempest*

# 1 The Search for GRIMALKIN

**W**HEN THE GALE swept over Ireland during Monday night, it seemed like any other summer storm that catches a few boats out in the Western Approaches to England. The wind built to thirty then forty knots. But it kept increasing, and by the time it reached fifty and more, the coastguards who watch over the 180-mile stretch of water between Land's End and Fastnet Rock knew they had a force 10 gale on their hands.

The distress calls increased in number as the wind strengthened. A yacht named *Regardless* lost her rudder before midnight, and the lifeboat based in Baltimore, Ireland, was dispatched to tow her in. Then *Wild Goose, Accanito,* and *Magic* sent out Maydays over marine radio frequencies, and by 3:00 A.M. (British Summer Time), on Tuesday morning, August 14, four lifeboats—three Irish and one English—were pounding over and through seas they reported as "very high" in search of half a dozen distressed yachts.

The people who live on either side of the Western Approaches are never surprised by bad weather, even during August, normally the warmest month of the year. Neither are they surprised by what wind and waves can do to ships and yachts. Yet as the airwaves became filled with Maydays and the sky over the Approaches was dotted with flares, the coastguards and lifeboat men stationed in the Irish Republic and in western Britain soon realized that a major disaster was developing that early morning. At 3:16 A.M., the Land's End Coastguard station requested help from the Southern Rescue Co-ordination Centre (SRCC) at Plymouth. The air force and naval officers at the SRCC were not at all surprised by the request; they had been

---

A Wessex helicopter hovers over *Camargue* as the yacht's skipper prepares to jump overboard to be rescued. *Royal Navy*

monitoring the distress frequencies and the weather was deteriorating. They also knew that many yachts—just how many they were not sure—were out in the Western Approaches participating in the 605-mile Fastnet race. The SRCC ordered that search and rescue airplanes and helicopters be brought to readiness for takeoff at dawn at the Kinloss and Culdrose air bases.

First light came slowly on that wind-torn, overcast morning, but by 5:30, the Culdrose Naval Air Station, near Helston in Cornwall, was vibrating with the whirl of blades and the whine of turbine engines. The first helicopter lifted off at 5:35, manned by the standby crew that is always within a few minutes of the base. Fifteen minutes later, another helicopter was aloft; its pilot and airmen had been called in from summer leave. Those two were followed by six more, some borrowed from bases as far away as Prestwick, Scotland.

By 6:30, three helicopters and a Nimrod search and rescue airplane, from Kinloss, were over the Western Approaches. Warm and dry, the helicopter crews monitored the radios and peered down at the broiling water, searching for yachts in trouble. Two hundred feet below them, in much less comfort, the crews of the lifeboats, of the fisheries protection vessel HMS *Angelsey,* and of the Dutch frigate *Overijssel* (the guard ship for the race since no British ship had been available) squinted through the stinging spray and cold, driving wind. Far above flew the Nimrod, which, with her battery of radios and tracking devices (its military function is to trace submarines), assumed the job of on-scene search commander. Its radios, with a range far greater than any of those below, were picking up panic-stricken voices from all over the Western Approaches. The distress calls overlapped with each other and gave confusingly similar messages: was it one boat or were there ten that had capsized, been dismasted, lost rudders or crews? And where were they? With twenty thousand square miles to cover, and with poor visibility, the rescuers were almost helpless.

For a while, only good luck brought the rescuers to the yachts in trouble. When they arrived, the helicopter crews discovered that many, if not most, of the crews wanted to abandon ship immediately. The helicopter crews are experts at their business, and their ability is legendary in Great Britain. In all of 1978, air-sea rescue helicopters based at Culdrose had saved one hundred and fifty people from sinking boats and ships, beaches, and cliffs.

"Can we be taken off?" a man in the French yacht *Tarantula* radioed to a helicopter.

"It won't be easy," the pilot responded.

Her crew thought *Tarantula* was sinking; they felt they had to abandon. Because the mast of the wildly rolling yacht was a menace to the retrieving cable, the airmen, hovering forty feet overhead, indicated that they could only pick people out of the water. One sailor quickly jumped overboard and swam away from the yacht. The helicopter crew dropped the cable and rescue harness to him, and, in his bulky life jacket, he struggled to fit into the sling as waves broke over him. After twenty minutes, he signaled to the airmen, who winched him up. Secured to the cable only by his tightly clenched hands, the sailor skimmed through the thirty-foot waves and was blown through a great arc by the sixty-knot wind until he was hauled into the chopper's cabin. Understandably discouraged by their shipmate's experience, the remainder of *Tarantula*'s crew decided to stay on board and risk sinking.

Shuttling back and forth from their base to the maelstrom, the helicopters were to rescue seventy-four sailors. Despite their extraordinary efforts, the airmen could not find a yacht named *Grimalkin*. By midmorning on Tuesday, the SRCC knew that more than three hundred yachts crewed by almost three thousand sailors were caught in the storm. Many boats were never heard from, either because they did not have radios or because they were lucky and safe. Others sent out distress calls and were quickly located; a few unfortunate boats radioed Mayday and were not found until they were beyond help.

At 6:00 A.M. Tuesday, a coastguard broadcast said, "Yacht *Grimalkin* capsized in position thirty miles north-west of Land's End." Before dawn, *Grimalkin* had sent out a Mayday and a position, and the message had been relayed to Land's End by a larger yacht (perhaps the seventy-seven-foot round-the-world racer *Condor of Bermuda*). At 6:30, Culdrose told a helicopter with the call sign Wessex-520 to fly over the reported position on its way to the Isles of Scilly, where five yachts were said to have dragged their anchors and gone ashore. Wessex-520 found nothing at "position thirty miles north-west of Land's End" and returned to Culdrose to refuel. At about the same time, the coastguards (which serve as the first alert in the British maritime rescue system) asked the St. Ives, Cornwall, lifeboat to launch in search of *Grimalkin*. En route to the reported position, the lifeboat was directed by the Nimrod airplane to the French yacht *Azenora II*, which was participating not in the Fastnet race but in a race for single-handed sailors from Ireland to Brittany. The lifeboat towed the little yacht and her one-man crew to St. Ives.

At 7:15, another Wessex helicopter, number 521, lifted off from Culdrose with orders to search for *Grimalkin*. About an hour later, its pilot reported, "Am not in communication with anyone. Returning to Culdrose." Clearly, *Grimalkin* was not in the position she had reported. Soon, a new position was given by somebody who had seen her in the middle of the Western Approaches: 50°50' north, 6°50' west—*sixty-five* miles north-west of Land's End.

Culdrose once again dispatched Wessex-520 to find *Grimalkin* and, if necessary, rescue her crew. But the helicopter first came across the dismasted and sinking yacht *Magic*, whose distress had been reported as early as 5:00 A.M. At about 10:30, *Magic*'s five crew members were hauled into the helicopter and flown to Culdrose, where they were taken to the sick bay, given hot baths, and put to bed.

A bit later, a Sea King-type helicopter, larger and faster than the Wessex type, picked three men out of a life raft. They said they had abandoned *Grimalkin*, leaving behind two dead or dying companions.

Meanwhile, Wessex-527 was flying three- and four-hour sorties out into the Approaches, returning to Culdrose for periods as brief as five minutes to refuel, change crews, and disembark survivors. At 11:20, the helicopter approached *Camargue*, a thirty-four-foot English sloop whose crew had endured a fearsome battering. At 8:45 A.M., she had been smashed by a wave that threw all men on deck overboard. Two were rolled back on deck by the same wave, but Wilf Gribble, who had been steering, was left hanging upside down over the transom, tangled in lifelines that had been broken under the impact of his flying body. Gribble crawled back aboard.

An hour later, a huge wave broke on her deck, threw Gribble and the steering wheel he was holding overboard, and rolled *Camargue* completely over, where she remained for several seconds before righting herself. Gribble again climbed back aboard over the transom, and he helped retrieve another man who was dragging in the water at the end of the rope tether of his safety harness. Arthur Moss, the boat's owner, was pulled through the water with such force that some of his clothes and his wristwatch were torn off.

*Camargue*'s crew had had enough; Moss sent a Mayday over marine radio. When the helicopter arrived, the men, realizing that they could not be picked off the yacht, went into the water one after another—some voluntarily, others pushed by Moss. As one man later said, "The idea of jumping in was appalling," but there was no other way to get off the yacht, which seemed to be foundering. Wessex-527 retrieved the men one at a time.

With the eight men of *Camargue*'s crew on board, the helicopter returned to Culdrose, refueled, and was back in the air fifteen minutes later. After several hours of fruitless searching, she refueled at the British Airways helicopter base on St. Mary's, in the Isles of Scilly, and headed west once more to resume the search.

Again short of fuel, Wessex-527 approached a racing yacht named *Golden Apple of the Sun*. An Irish boat (her name is from a poem by Yeats), she was one of the stars of the 1979 yacht racing summer. With a crew that included a three-time Olympic yachting medalist, Rodney Pattison, and her celebrated de-

OVERLEAF: **The helicopter drops a hook to an airman and a *Camargue* crew member.** *Royal Navy*

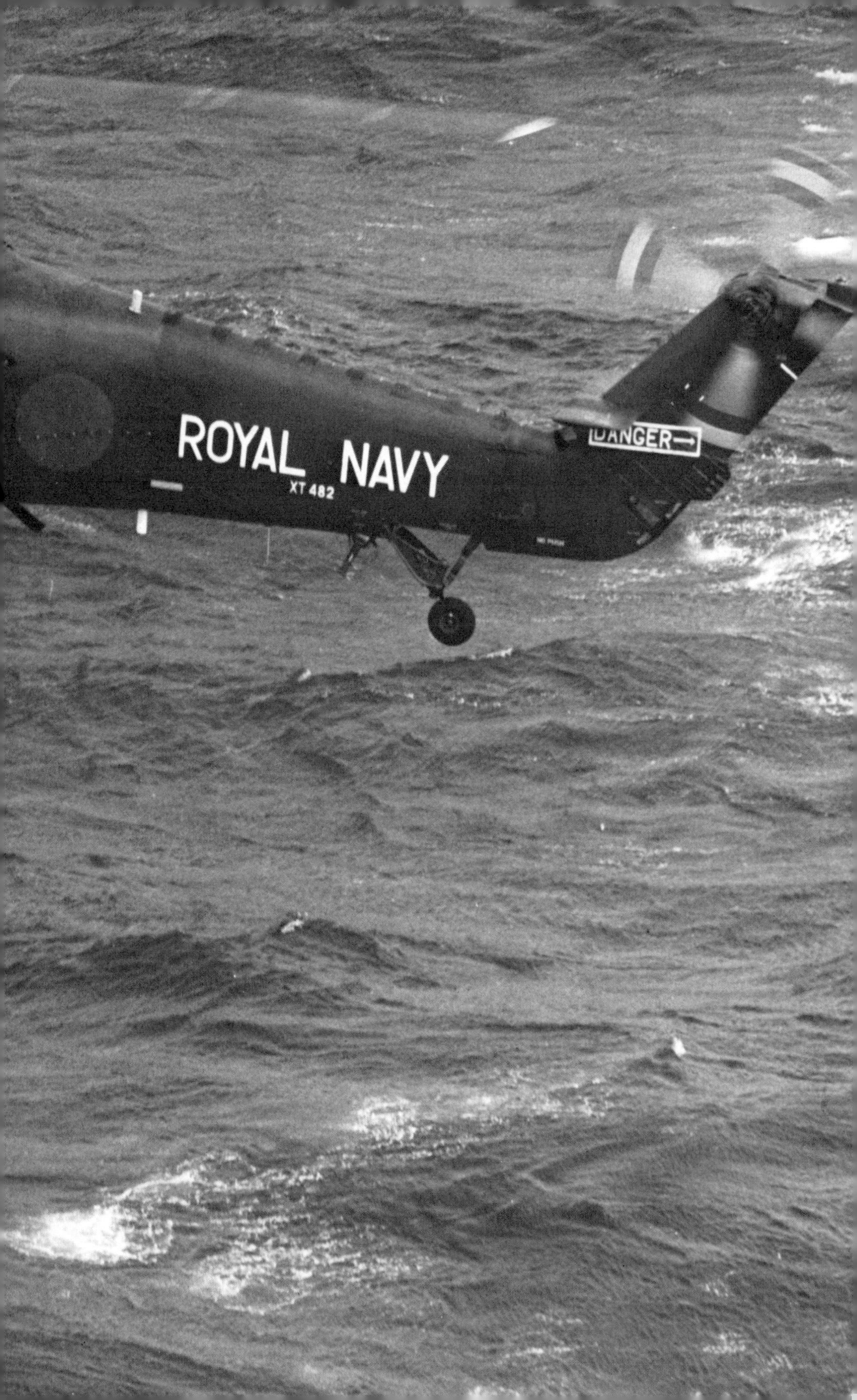
ROYAL NAVY
XT 482
DANGER

signer, Ron Holland, this forty-three-footer was a member of the three-boat Irish team competing in the Admiral's Cup, an unofficial world championship of ocean racing that includes the Fastnet as its major race. Coming into the Fastnet race, the Irish had been leading the eighteen other competing countries, but the race had been their undoing. One member of the Irish team, *Regardless*, had lost her rudder, and now *Golden Apple of the Sun* was also rudderless. Early that morning, the cables had jumped off the rudder quadrant, and the crew had lowered the sails for two hours to make repairs. They got under way again, but a couple of hours later, Ron Holland, who was at the helm, completely lost control. The rudder had broken off.

The crew had planned for such an emergency. They screwed a metal plate to the end of the spinnaker pole and hung the pole over the stern to serve as an emergency tiller. But the spinnaker pole almost immediately broke. Depressed as only a sure winner-turned-loser can be, the wet, cold crew hung on to the violently rolling boat. They were made no happier by hearing a radio report that a man was lost and presumed drowned from another racing yacht, *Festina Tertia*.

A helicopter, Wessex-527, appeared on the horizon, quickly approached, and hovered overhead. By radio, its pilot told *Golden Apple of the Sun*'s owner, Hugh Coveney, that he would have to make up his mind quickly about abandoning. With the Scilly Isles only forty miles to leeward, Coveney decided to go ashore and charter a powerboat to return to tow *Golden Apple* to port. Some of the crew disagreed, but the navigation lights were turned on, a radar reflector was hoisted, and bumpers were hung over the side. This was partly to protect her against collision with other vessels, partly to discourage would-be salvagers, who by law could lay claim to the yacht if her crew abandoned her with no plans to return.

Coveney decided to paddle out from the boat in the life raft. Its $CO_2$ cartridge was triggered, but the raft inflated only partially. When it was dropped in the water, its bowline immediately parted, but a crew member managed to grab it before it drifted away. The entire ten-man crew did not fit into the raft, so some men had to lie across others. When they were all aboard, the raft did not float away from *Golden Apple,* which threatened to roll over on its awkwardly seated crew. Seeing this risk, the helicopter's diver, Leading Aircrewman Smiler Grinney, dropped down from the Wessex, swam over, and pulled the near awash raft away from the yacht, and the pilot helped by aiming the downdraft between the vessels. The sailors were hauled, one by one, into the helicopter.

*Grimalkin* still had not been found as the eighteen men rescued by Wessex-527 and the dozens more picked up by the seven other helicopters recovered from their ordeal in the Culdrose sick bay. When Sea King-590 took off at 6:30, it was on one of the last missions of the day. It had flown down from Prestwick, Scotland, Tuesday morning. This was the first mission for one of her two winchmen, Peter Harrison, a twenty-year-old midshipman who had only recently completed two years of training in air-sea rescue.

After two hours of patrolling, the crew spotted a dismasted white yacht with a black transom on which was written: "*Grimalkin,* Southampton, RAFYC." Two motionless men were sprawled in her cockpit. Peter Harrison stepped into the sling, and in his helmet, overalls, life jacket, and emergency pack, which included an uninflated two-man life raft, he was lowered to the yacht by the winch operator. *Grimalkin* rose on a wave to meet him, and he hit her deck with a bone-crushing thud.

Harrison picked himself up and looked around the deck of the wildly rolling yacht. She was a mess, with bits of mast, rigging, and sails strewn everywhere. He turned to the two men and told them that they had little time: it was getting dark, the helicopter could not wait, they had to abandon now.

One of the men, the younger one, seemed not to be listening. With tears pouring down his cheeks, he said, over and over again, "I must get my clothes." The other man, lying in the bottom of the cockpit, said nothing. It took a moment for Harrison to realize that the other man was dead.

# 2 GRIMALKIN: An Orderly Boat, a Disorderly Storm

THE ABANDONMENT OF *Grimalkin* was also the abandonment of high hopes. David Sheahan, her owner, was one of thousands of middle-class people who were attracted to the sport of ocean racing, looking for escape from the pressures of organized, professional life ashore. Fastnet race fleets had doubled in size since the late 1960s, and the sport boomed everywhere as more disposable income and leisure time became available to an increasing number of people. Away from land for several days at a time, fighting the weather and the sea in relatively small sailboats, men and women could regain touch with the satisfactions of working together in a natural environment—satisfactions that were a part of normal everyday existence before work became stratified, individualized, and air-conditioned.

The virtues of the discomfort of an ocean-racing yacht—wet clothes, lack of sleep, bunk sharing, and the constant pressure to outrace frequently invisible competitors—are difficult to explain yet addictive. For the men and women who keep returning to the Fastnet and other long-distance races until they are on the verge of old age, the lure is not the hope of winning trophies. Perhaps the sport provides a means of rediscovering some lost part of their primitive nature, unsullied by civilized life. In the 1970s, yachting went through a technological revolution as space-age materials and electronic instruments found their way into boats that were becoming increasingly fast and difficult to sail well. Many younger sailors seemed to respond to these challenging developments with the enthusiastic delight of race-car drivers and mechanics first encountering turbocharged engines, and the satisfactions of sailing in an ocean race may

---

PRECEDING PHOTOGRAPH: *Grimalkin* racing under number-2 jib and single-reefed mainsail in a force 5 (seventeen- to twenty-one-knot) breeze before the Fastnet race.

have been less important in their minds to the pleasures of winning. Yet for most of the twenty-seven or so people in the 1979 Fastnet race, the attractions of the sport were the same ones that had encouraged ninety men to sail in nine yachts in the first Fastnet race, in 1925.

Like a great many of the people in the 303 boats that started the Fastnet race on August 11, David Sheahan had only recently discovered ocean racing. An accountant in his early forties, he had raced in dinghies and other day-sailing boats for many years before buying *Grimalkin*. Thirty feet long, she was almost the minimum size for most of the important distance races sailed off England, but she had a pedigree. Her designer was Ron Holland, in the past five years probably the most successful architect of ocean-racing yachts. She was built of fiberglass by the distinguished English firm of Camper and Nicholsons. Her shape, construction, rigging, and equipment were as modern as those of most of her competitors. Sheahan did his best to supplement his boat's inherent speed and strengths with careful organization for the many races he entered. Some boat owners set aside the conscious, orderly sides of their natures when they make the transition from work to pleasure, but he approached yachting with the same attention to detail that he showed in his profession.

The six-page memorandum that Sheahan sent to his crew before the Fastnet race began with a description of the course. The race would start in the early afternoon on August 11 off the Royal Yacht Squadron, at Cowes, on the Isle of Wight. The course was 605 miles long: from Cowes down the southwest coast and around Land's End; across the Western Approaches and around Fastnet Rock, which lies eight miles off the southwest tip of Ireland; then back to England and around the Isles of Scilly and on to the finish at Plymouth. *Grimalkin* would sail in Class V, reserved for the smallest boats, and she might be at sea for more than six days.

Sheahan then reported that the safety gear, which included a rubber life raft inflatable by a $CO_2$ cartridge, flares, and equipment to aid in the rescue of crew members who had gone over-

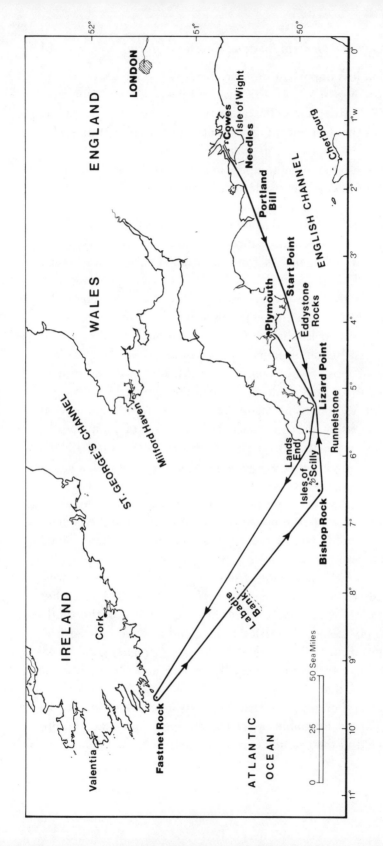

The 605-mile Fastnet race course. Shown are the main headlands and turning points. On the way out to Fastnet Rock, the Isles of Scilly may be passed on either side, but on the way back from the Western Approaches, they must be passed to the south.

board, would be examined by Camper and Nicholsons. They would also make a repair to the yacht's rudder. He planned to carry six gallons of diesel fuel, enough to run the engine for twenty-four hours in order to charge batteries and "to give ourselves a safety margin in case of problems." And, he wrote, "The insurance of the boat and its contents (i.e., the crew) has been extended to take in this race, which is beyond our normal cruising (*sic!*) limits." *Grimalkin* never went on cruises, and her normal insurance applied only near her home waters, on the Solent near Hamble. Sheahan then discussed safety. Although the first-aid kit would be "upgraded to a more suitable level for this event," each crew member was responsible for his own special medication. He recommended that each make an appointment for a prerace dental checkup, and flatly reported that nobody on board had special medical training.

Since space was limited in the little boat (food would be stored in clothing lockers), everybody was expected to bring aboard only one duffel of sailing clothes. Shore clothes, Sheahan ironically noted, would not be necessary "as we will break with our normal tradition and not dress for cocktails or dinner."

As for provisions, Sheahan expected the crew to share equally in the cost of food, for which he and a crew member, Gerry Winks, would shop. Although he had increased *Grimalkin*'s water capacity to twenty-five gallons, Sheahan wrote, washing and cooking would be done in sea water, and to provide a reserve for emergencies, fresh-water consumption would be limited to three gallons a day. He asked the crew to notify him if there were special dietary problems.

Continuing with his concern about emergencies, Sheahan noted that he planned to talk daily over marine radio with his wife, who would be able to transmit any messages to families. "It might not always be possible," he cautioned, "so make sure that your family, etc., don't worry unduly if there is no news to pass on."

Taking almost an entire page, Sheahan detailed the crew assignments. He would be skipper and navigator; Gerry Winks would be second in command; Mike Doyle would back Sheahan up "to ensure that in all circumstances we have a navigator"; his seventeen-year-old son, Matthew, would be in charge of the foredeck and sail changes; Nick Ward would trim the spinnaker; and Dave Wheeler would help Matthew on the foredeck. They would all take turns steering and cooking. *Grimalkin's* watch system, described in the memorandum in a two-page chart, had two men on deck at all times. Each of the five men who stood watch (Sheahan would be busy navigating) would alternate four hours on deck and four hours below, and during the race each would take one twelve-hour period off the watch schedule to cook.

Sheahan ended his memorandum with instructions to be aboard *Grimalkin* at 8:00 A.M. on the eleventh and with a final reminder: "We have maintained a high standard of personal safety on board, let's retain it for this event."

Although no skipper preparing for the Fastnet race should have been unaware of the potential for bad weather—strong winds often are as much a part of sailing off the English coast as light winds are prevalent on Long Island Sound in America —Sheahan's relative lack of experience may have made him more cautious than many Fastnet race veterans. The previous three races, in 1973, 1975, and 1977, had been sailed in light winds and calms in which the main worry had been food and water shortage, not first-aid equipment.

Safety harnesses that restrain crew members from being flung overboard, life jackets and life rafts, fire extinguishers, first-aid kits, emergency rations—all were required of Fastnet race entrants by the sponsor, the Royal Ocean Racing Club (RORC). Yet a man who worries about whether his crew will suffer toothaches is not a man to take chances. The RORC did not require Sheahan to carry a radio transmitter. A receiver capable of picking up marine weather broadcasts was the only radio that *Grimalkin* and most of the other Fastnet entrants had to have aboard. (The exceptions were the fifty-seven boats in the Admiral's Cup competition, which were required to carry transmitters. In 1979, the Admiral's Cup, an international championship for ocean racers sailed biennially in Fastnet race years, included three-boat teams from nineteen nations, among them the United States, Poland, Hong Kong, Brazil, Ireland, Australia, and Great Britain.) Even though he was not required to do so, Sheahan equipped *Grimalkin* with three very high frequency (VHF) marine radio transmitters and receivers, two of which were powered by the boat's battery, and one of which could be used in a life raft if necessary.

Sheahan also went beyond the regulations to equip his boat with jackwires along the decks and in the cockpit (in nautical parlance, "jack" means "utility"). In rough weather, his crew could hook the snap hooks at the end of the six-foot tethers on their safety harnesses to these wires so they would be securely attached to the boat as they worked on deck or sat in the cockpit. The racing regulations required only that *Grimalkin* be equipped with lifelines running fore and aft two feet above each rail, suspended on stainless-steel posts called stanchions. Both the stanchions and lifelines were vulnerable to damage by a broken mast or by a man thrown against them, and Sheahan felt that, in the worst possible situation, the jackwires were more dependable restraints against a man's being flung into the sea.

David Sheahan's concern for safety may have been motivated by knowledge that his crew was, in a way, flawed. Gerry Winks, the first mate, was arthritic, and Nick Ward, the sail trimmer, was an epileptic. Neither case was serious, and with the proper medication the two men were able to lead normally active lives. Yet doctors had advised Winks not to sail. He ignored that advice. At age thirty-five, Gerry Winks aspired to being a successful yachtsman with all the eagerness of a young boy hoping to score goals in a soccer World Cup. His spare time was devoted to boats: sailing in them, reading about them in books and yachting magazines, planning for the day when he could be skipper of his own ocean racer in a Fastnet race. "The Fastnet is either the beginning or the end," he told his wife before setting out in *Grimalkin*. "I'll know myself as a racing yachtsman after this." If he proved himself by meeting his own high standards in this race, he would try to join the crew of a larger boat, and then onwards until he could afford his own yacht—regardless of doctor's orders. But until then, he would do his best to help David Sheahan win in *Grimalkin*.

When Nick Ward was sixteen, he suffered a neurological attack that left him partially paralyzed. Technically an epileptic, he had little or no feeling in his left side, although he was able, with medication, to stay active, ride his bicycle, and continue sailing dinghies. He took waterfront jobs in boatyards, marinas, and chandleries, and by the time he was twenty-four, he had helped deliver many yachts across the English Channel and the Bay of Biscay and had endured bad weather offshore. His knowledge, experience, seriousness, and intensity made him a valued member of racing crews. David Sheahan sought him out and asked him to come aboard *Grimalkin* for the 1979 racing season. His only failing afloat was clumsiness in the galley. While cooking during a race in the Channel, he allowed a plastic spatula to melt in a frying pan. Sheahan, who knew the importance of barracks humor to a group of men under pressure, turned the incident into a running joke, announcing in the pre-Fastnet race memorandum that Ward was scheduled to take the first tour as cook just after the start "whilst we still have a packed lunch," and labeling the new spatula "The Nick Ward Memorial."

*Grimalkin*'s crew members were in high spirits when they boarded her at Hamble, near Southampton, early in the warm, sunny morning of August 11. They stowed their seabags and cast off the dock lines, and as *Grimalkin* made her way under power out toward Cowes, they sang loudly and waved cheerily to friends on the pier. Margaret Winks, Gerry's wife, was there to send them off, and the possibility of danger never crossed her

---

ON THE FOLLOWING PAGES: Like *Grimalkin* and other boats in the race, *Toscana* was rigged with jackwires that ran the length of each deck and a crew member could go all the way forward to the bow without having to unclip his safety harness • Since a crew member coming on deck is not sturdily supported, he should pass the tether and hook over the washboards to another crew member, who may hook it to a jackwire • The helmsman must be securely hooked to the jackwire. On many boats rolled during the night, helmsmen were thrown from the tiller or wheel right over the lifelines. This jackwire was permanently rigged in the cockpit on *Innovation*, whose owner, Peter Johnson, here demonstrates its use. *John Rousmaniere*

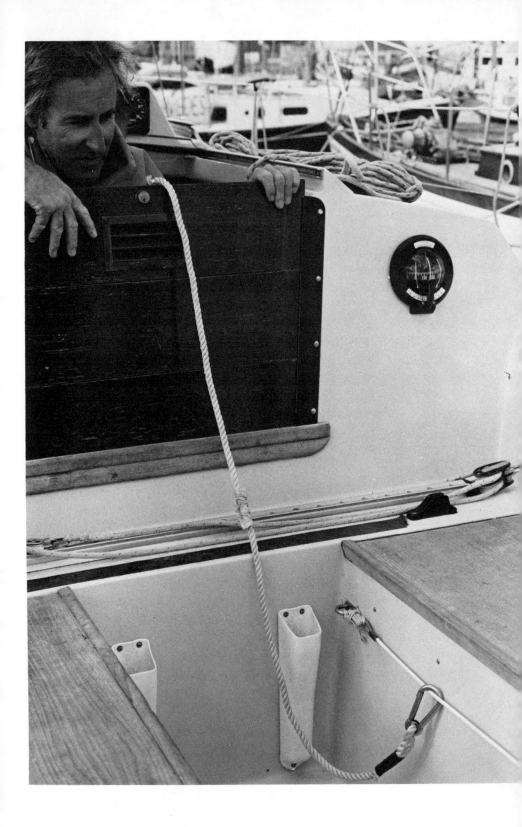

mind as she watched the boat and her crew head off into the light south-west breeze.

Class V was the first group to start from the line that extended from transits on the castlelike clubhouse of the Royal Yacht Squadron to an outer distance buoy over one mile out in the Solent, the narrow body of water that separates the Isle of Wight from the English mainland. Fifty-eight boats crossed the line in Class V, while the 245 larger boats in Classes O, I, II, III, and IV, and a flock of photographer, press, and spectator boats swarming about, somehow avoided collision. A strong tidal stream pushing the boats toward and over the starting line further confused the situation. Sheahan was not intimidated. *Grimalkin* had an excellent start and held her own against larger boats as she tacked to windward, working her way toward the Needles, the chalk cliffs that guard the west end of the Solent.

The south-west wind held steady for the next two days, rarely blowing less than ten or more than fifteen knots as the massive fleet of racing yachts sailed as closely as they could in its direction, first on one tack and then, after a wind shift of a few degrees, on another. The sea was calm and the only discomfort was the minor annoyance of living in a world that was tilted twenty degrees. *Grimalkin* encouraged her crew by continuing to sail near boats ten to fifteen feet longer and potentially much faster as most of the huge fleet sailed close along the English shore to try to avoid strong contrary currents. David Sheahan endured the bout of seasickness that often afflicts even highly experienced offshore sailors on their first day or so at sea. When he recovered, he used one of the radios to call a marine operator, who connected him to his home telephone, and he told his wife that they were comfortable and sailing fast.

Like most of the Fastnet race entries, *Grimalkin*'s crew depended for weather forecasts on the British Broadcasting Corporation's four times daily shipping bulletin on the long-range Radio 4. The forecasts had been almost exactly the same since Friday: southwesterlies of force 4 to force 5, with the chance of a force 7 or force 8 gale near Fastnet Rock on Monday, the thirteenth. In the Beaufort scale of wind and sea conditions, used by most seamen and yachtsmen to describe the weather, force 4 ("Moderate Breeze") is an average of eleven to sixteen knots of wind (one knot is equal to 1.1 miles per hour), so the lower ranges of the forecast certainly were correct; only occasionally did the fleet feel the seventeen to twenty-one knots of wind of force 5 ("Fresh Breeze"). Force 7 ("Moderate Gale") and force 8 ("Fresh Gale") encompass wind strengths of between twenty-eight and forty knots, which every sailor in *Grimalkin* and her competitors must have experienced at least once in their sailing careers, and, which, probably, they all desired for at least part of this Fastnet race.

The forecasts duly came at 12:15 A.M., 6:25 A.M., 1:55 P.M., and 5:50 P.M., and the wind and the barometer held steady at the relatively high pressure of 1020 millibars (30.1 inches), yet the thick fog that shrouded the boats most of Sunday was not evidence of the kind of stable fair weather that those indicators normally point to. The fog cleared away Sunday night and was replaced just after dawn on Monday by a flat calm. The air sat motionless between thick puffy clouds and a greasy sea undulating monotonously to the rhythms of the groundswell that rolls in soundlessly from the Atlantic. The groundswell is propelled by the southwesterlies that are ubiquitous except when a cell of low atmospheric pressure, called a depression, sweeps east from America to cancel out the effects of the great stable Azores high-pressure system. *Grimalkin* rolled uncomfortably in these waves as her crew looked aloft for any indication of wind in the sails. After several hours, a breeze filled in quickly from a new direction—the north-east—and her crew soon had *Grimalkin* decked out in a spinnaker to take advantage of the new wind from astern. As she cleared Land's End and stuck her bow out into the Western Approaches, she was propelled at eight knots, almost twice the speed she had been making on the two-day, 210-mile leg into the wind down from Cowes.

Once again, the thirty-footer was staying even with larger

boats, and her crew had every reason to feel satisfied. But for
those who looked up into the western sky early Monday afternoon, there were other things to think about. The clouds were
darkening to the point where Nick Ward thought them "terrific." The barometer had dropped slightly, to 1010 millibars
(29.8 inches), and, with the strengthening wind that was slowly
veering from north-east to east to south-east, there was reason to
suspect that some bad weather was on the way. Yet the 1:55 P.M.
BBC shipping bulletin for sea area Fastnet was: "south-westerly,
force 4 or 5, increasing 6 or 7 for a time, veering westerly later.
Occasional rain or showers." That said only that a depression
would be passing through with no more wind than had previously been forecast, but with a shift in wind direction to the
west. Despite the clouds and the groundswell, which seemed to
be growing higher, there was little in the wind or over the radio frequencies to cause even the most cautious sailor to con-
sider turning back and heading for a protected harbor.

By late Monday afternoon, the wind had shifted to the south-
west and had increased to twenty knots, with occasional puffs of
twenty-five. *Grimalkin*'s crew doused her spinnaker, and, heading west-northwest toward Fastnet Rock, she burst over and
sometimes through the swells at exhilarating speeds, under
mainsail and genoa jib. At 5:50 P.M. the precise yet sympathetic
voice of the BBC announcer presented the shipping bulletin,
the relevant part of which was, "Mainly southerly 4 locally 6, increasing 6 locally gale 8, becoming mainly north-westerly later."
He also located a depression two hundred and fifty miles west of
the Fastnet area that the British meteorological office expected
to pass to the north.

The six men in *Grimalkin* were not surprised by this news,
for it was not the first mention of a force 8 gale. Yet a forecast
two hours later from another source painted a new and much
more worrisome picture. At about 8:00 P.M., a French-language
broadcast anticipated a force 8 to force 10 gale, with stronger
gusts. Called a "Whole Gale" or "Storm" in the Beaufort scale,
force 10 conditions are considerably more severe than force 8.
Force 10's forty-eight- to fifty-five-knot winds are some twenty

knots stronger, and its thirty-two- to forty-foot waves are as much as twice as high. Most significant is the violence of force 10 waves. The description in the Beaufort scale is "Very high waves with long overhanging crests. The resulting foam in great patches is blown in dense white streaks along the direction of the wind. On the whole the surface of the sea takes a white appearance. The tumbling of the sea becomes heavy and shock-like. Visibility affected."

The maelstrom described in those five sentences and phrases is entirely more vicious than a force 8 sea, in which there are "Moderately high waves of greater length [than force 7 waves]; edges of crests begin to break into spindrift. The foam is blown in well-marked streaks along the direction of the wind." Force 10 is to force 8 what stomach cancer is to gallstones.

David Sheahan and his crew knew the difference between force 10 and force 8, and the French broadcast worried them. *Grimalkin*, it seemed, was now heading straight into a major storm. Another Fastnet race boat, later remembered as *Pegasus*, also heard the forecast, and her crew called the Land's End Coastguard station over her marine radio to ask if the French had been correct. By the rules of yacht racing, this was illegal, since *Pegasus* was soliciting outside help, but the action is understandable given the circumstances. The coastguards' response was that the BBC forecast was the correct one. Overhearing both the question and the answer, *Grimalkin*'s crew breathed more easily. Yet the barometer had dropped to 995 millibars (29.4 inches), the wind had increased to thirty knots, the waves were building in size, and the boat was beginning to pound uncomfortably. The sun set at 8:26, its rays mostly hidden by low scuddy black clouds flying over water now broken by spray and whitecaps.

David Sheahan could not know that the French forecast had been accurate. *Grimalkin* was about to rendezvous with a compact, violent storm that had traveled over five thousand miles in four days to sweep across the Western Approaches during the precise hours when those waters would be crowded with small racing yachts.

"Depressions are born, reach maturity, and then decline and die," the English weather specialist Ingrid Holford writes in *The Yachtsman's Weather Guide.* "They travel in their youth and stagnate in their retirement; some are feeble from birth and never make a mark on the world, while others attain a vigor which makes them remembered with as much awe as a hurricane." This storm had already made its mark.

The storm was born in the northern Great Plains of the United States, where hot air over baking wheat fields frequently tangles with cold Canadian air to produce tornadoes and violent thunderstorms. Often, these tiny, vicious depressions do their worst damage immediately and are quickly gone, their energy dissipated in wind, rain, and hail. But this storm had a force that kept it alive long after it dropped over an inch and a half of rain on Minneapolis, Minnesota, on Thursday, August 9. From there it headed east across northern Lake Michigan, upstate New York, and New England. Its greatest effects were to its south. On Friday, sixty-knot wind gusts blew the roof off a tollbooth on the New Jersey Turnpike and knocked down power lines and tree limbs, one of which killed a woman walking in Central Park, in New York City. That afternoon, severe wind and rain squalls swept across Connecticut and into Narragansett Bay, in Rhode Island, where the twelve-meter yacht *Intrepid* was practicing for the 1980 America's Cup trials. One of her wire jib sheets broke and hit a crew member with such force that he thought his arm was broken. Nearby, seventy-eight boats competing in the world championship of the J-24 sailboat class were swept by unpredictable, violent gusts from the south-west and north-west. Three boats were knocked over until their masts touched the water. The boats finished the race under a black sky and made it safely into the protected harbor of Newport just before the Coast Guard issued an alert warning all sailors to seek shelter. Sheets of rain drenched the town, and a fifty-knot wind broke windows and threatened to blow over a large waterside tent. One sailor, Mary Johnstone, thought that this thirty-minute period of rain and wind was as wild as some of the hurricanes she had experienced during her many years of living in

New England. That night, northwest squalls swept across the crowded harbors of the islands off southern New England, and dozens of yachts containing vacationers dragged their anchors. Moving east at speeds as high as fifty knots, the swirling cell of violent air was over Halifax, Nova Scotia, at about the time the Fastnet race started on Saturday, and was in the open Atlantic a day later.

So small and fast moving was the storm that meteorologists had difficulty keeping a precise track of it, and some of the weather maps compiled every six hours by the United States National Weather Service show it only as an area of low pressure and not as a distinct depression encircled by isobars, or lines of equal barometric pressure. The weather map published in British newspapers over the August 11–12 weekend identified the depression as "Low Y" that would "move quickly east and deepen" to cause the force 7 winds predicted for Monday.

In meteorologists' terminology, this was a "shallow" depression with an atmospheric pressure of about 1008 millibars (29.8 inches) at the lowest. A "deep" depression might have a pressure of less than 995 millibars (29.4 inches). Differences in atmospheric pressure are what create weather and, in particular, wind. Hot air and damp air are less dense than cool air and dry air. The less dense air has a lower pressure than the dense air and creates depressions in the atmosphere in the way a prolonged rainfall creates valleys and basins in a beach. Into these depressions pours cooler, more dense air from surrounding high-pressure hilltops or plateaus: the deeper the depression, the steeper the slope of the hill; the steeper the slope, the faster the air moves and the more wind there is.

Due to the earth's rotation, this flow of air from high to low pressure is not straight. The Coriolis effect curves the flow to the right, or counterclockwise, in the northern hemisphere and to the left in the southern hemisphere. In the northern hemisphere, air flows toward the center of a depression in the same way that water drains out of a sink, spinning in a counterclockwise direction as it works its way to the center. The deeper the depression, the more rapid the spin. The flow takes a different compass direction at each point on the spiral. To the north of a depression, the wind blows from the north-east; to the west, from the north-west; to the east, from the south-east; and to the south, from the south-west.

Depressions, unlike sinks, are usually in motion, being pushed from west to east by the prevailing westerlies created by the spin of the earth. A phenomenon of depressions is that when they move slowly they are relatively benign, but when they move rapidly they may be more dangerous than the differences of atmospheric pressure indicate. To put it another way, a fast-moving shallow depression may be more violent than a slow-moving deeper depression. Another phenomenon of depressions, especially the fast-moving ones, is that the winds on their lower half—the southern part of a depression moving east—may well be more violent than those on the upper half. In fact, sailors often speak of a storm's "dangerous quadrant," its lower right-hand area. As people in New Jersey, New York, and Rhode Island already knew, the winds in the lower half of this particular fast-moving depression were exceedingly violent.

Between midday Sunday (as *Grimalkin* sailed down the English Channel in the fog) and midday Monday (when the north-east wind filled in after the calm), the depression traveled east-northeast at a speed of between twenty and forty knots, covering over eight hundred miles. To its south was the great Azores high, a mass of air with relatively high atmospheric pressures in the range of 1017 to 1034 millibars (30.0 to 30.5 inches). Air flowed down the slopes of this nearly stationary mid-Atlantic mound into the valleys of the low-pressure areas around it. The Coriolis effect of the spin of the earth redirected this air to the right, so that to the north of the Azores high a southwest wind was helping to push Low Y toward the north-east.

Conspiring with the high was a large depression of low-pressure air to the north that stretched almost one thousand miles from the latitude of Greenland to the latitude of northern Ireland. The depression had left the coast of Canada on Friday morning, the tenth, and had lumbered across the Labrador Banks, absorbing along the way two smaller depressions that had moved down from Greenland. On Sunday morning, August 12, the center of this depression was located about three hundred and fifty miles south-west of Reykjavik, Iceland. Called "Low X" on British weather maps (since it had been spotted earlier than the depression called Low Y), it had an atmospheric pressure of 990 millibars (29.2 inches) and perhaps a bit less in its center. The outer isobar of Low X, 1016 millibars (30.0 inches), stretched across the mid-Atlantic Ocean between the latitudes of fifty and sixty degrees north. The wind there also blew from the south-west.

Low Y had hitchhiked east on the westerlies of the Azores high and Low X. Born at the latitude of forty-five degrees, the depression had not moved south of forty-three nor north of forty-seven degrees during its quick trip across eastern America and the western Atlantic, and it would have made its European landfall in the Bay of Biscay if another factor had not appeared.

This factor was offered by Low X. Instead of continuing on its easterly course, Low X stopped moving. While it stalled for two days off the west coast of Iceland, Low Y overtook it and moved into the quadrant where southerlies and not westerlies blew. In the predawn hours of Monday, August 13, the dangerous little depression changed course and headed northeast, at first aimed west of Ireland on the well-worn path of many previous depressions. Once weather satellites had a look at it and computers could digest the limited amount of information that was radioed from a few ships in mid-Atlantic, the British forecasters realized at around noon on Monday that Low Y, swinging around Low X, would sweep across southern Ireland and the Western Approaches that night.

Unfortunately, the meteorological office came to this conclusion too late to provide a gale warning for the 1:55 P.M. BBC Radio 4 shipping bulletin, upon which almost all the Fastnet race sailors depended for their afternoon weather forecast. The forecasters did, however, issue for special broadcast a warning of an imminent force 8 gale for southern Ireland and the Fastnet area ("imminent" meaning within the next six hours) and for a force 8 gale expected soon at Lundy, the island at the

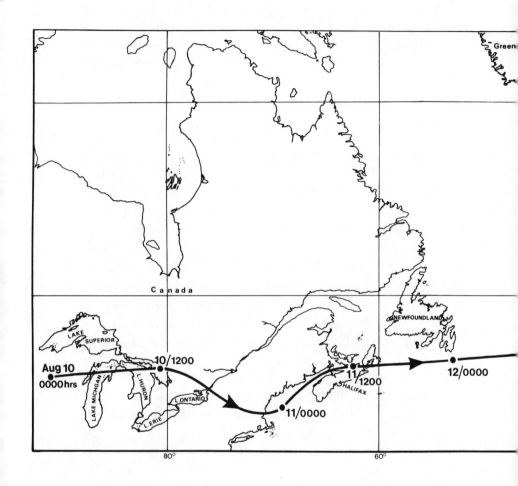

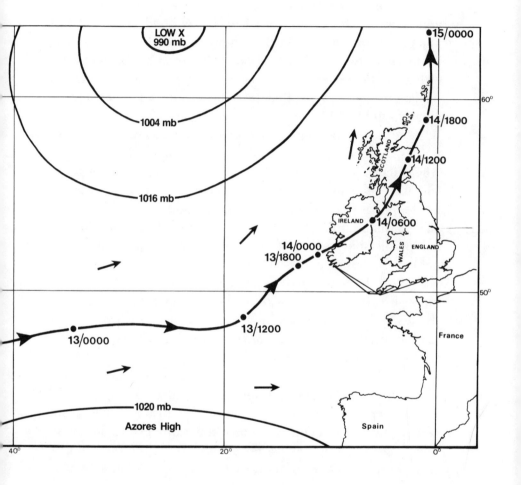

The path of Low Y from its start in Minnesota on August 10, until it died out north of Scotland on August 15. Low Y began to move north-eastwards toward Ireland only after it overtook Low X, which had stalled far to the north off Iceland. The westerlies created by Low X and by the Azores high (to the south) helped to push Low Y east at speeds as high as fifty knots. The arrows show wind direction. Times are Greenwich Mean Time.

mouth of the Bristol Channel and one hundred miles north-
east of Land's End ("expected soon" meaning from six to
twelve hours after the forecast).

Made even more violent by cold air sweeping down into it
from Low X, the depression slowed down and deepened on
Monday afternoon, and the 5:50 shipping bulletin reported that
it was about two hundred and fifty miles west of Fastnet Rock
with a barometric pressure of 998 millibars (29.5 inches). Again
too late for the shipping bulletin, which would not come on the
air again until 12:15 A.M., the meteorological office at 6:05 P.M.
released a new warning of imminent force 8 increasing to force
9 gales in the Fastnet area. If they had continuously monitored
BBC's Radio 4 or if they had been within the limited range of
and had been listening to one of four coastal radio stations
using special frequencies, the sailors would have heard these
gale warnings. But being human, they relied upon scheduled
and predictable sources of information, and most of them had
neither the time nor the inclination to monitor radios continuously. Furthermore, radios can be a drain on batteries that
must also be used to provide power for navigation lights. (In
the United States, many areas are covered by continuous
marine weather forecasts, which are repeated every few minutes on special frequencies.)

At 8:50 P.M., the meteorological office issued revised gale
warnings for mainland Ireland: the imminent force 9 winds
would veer from south-west to west. The area that most concerned any racing sailors who heard the warnings was not men-
tioned again in new gale warnings until 10:45: "Fastnet: south-
west severe gale force 9 increasing storm force 10 imminent."

---

Satellite photographs on the following pages show the eastern North Atlantic at approximately 4:50 P.M. (British Summer Time) on Sunday, August 12  •  Monday, August
13  •  and Tuesday, August 14  •  The Fastnet race course has been imposed. The photographs show Low X—the large swirl of clouds in the upper center—stalled off Iceland,
and, to its south, Low Y approaching Great Britain and swinging across Scotland and over
the North Sea. The second photograph was taken at about the time that weathermen
realized that Low Y would sweep across the Fastnet fleet. U.S. National Oceanographic
and Atmospheric Administration

70N·020W 1552

60N·020W 1549

50N·010W 1546

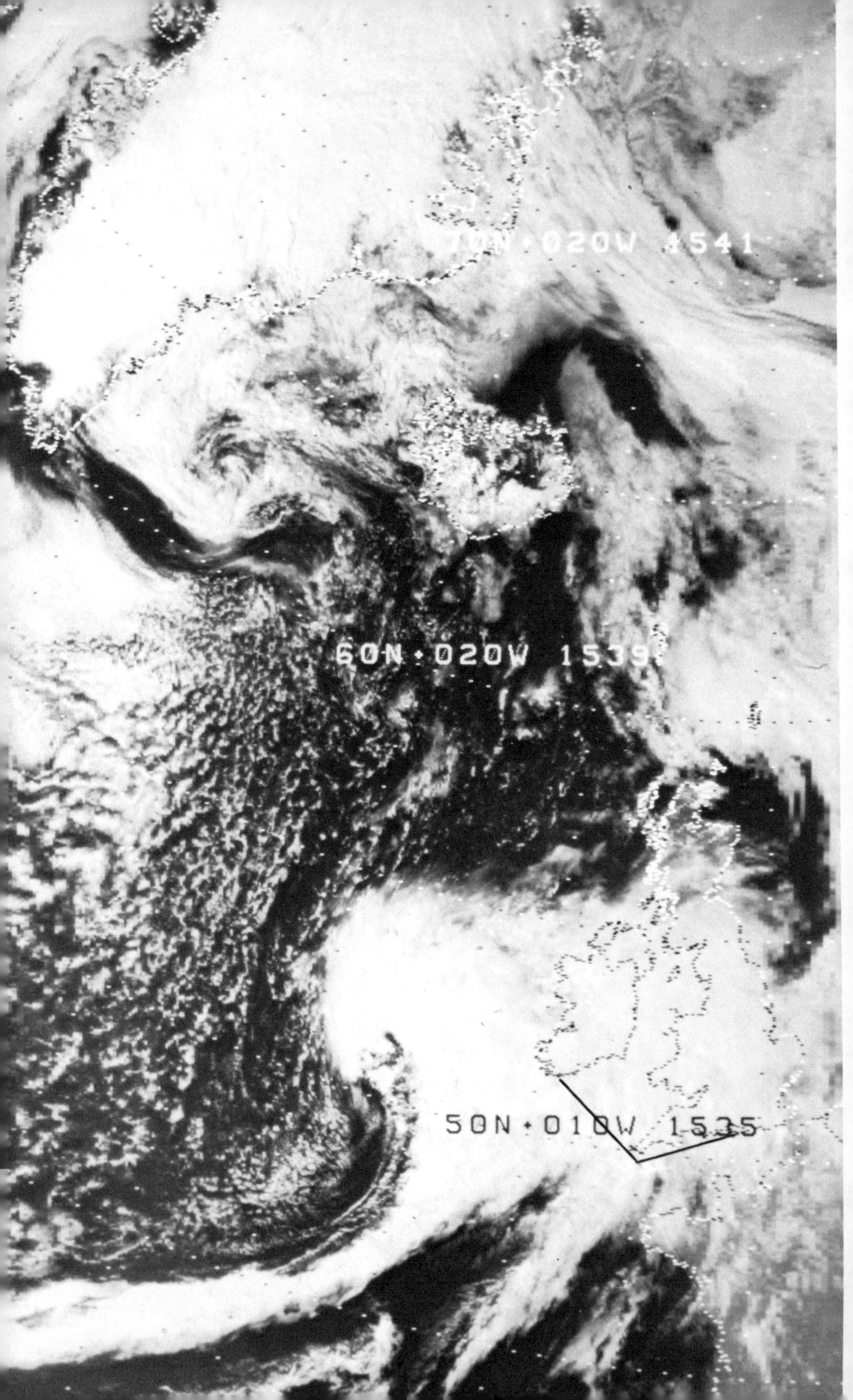
70N 020W 1541
60N 020W 1539
50N 010W 1535

70N·000E 1349

50N·010E 1346

50N·020E 1343

During its weather forecast that evening, BBC television showed a satellite picture of the Atlantic Ocean west of Ireland. The photograph was dominated by a clearly defined swirl of clouds curving north about three hundred miles south-west of Ireland. This was the front of the depression. Erroll Bruce, an experienced ocean-racing sailor who was sitting out this Fastnet race, took one look at the picture and telephoned his business partner Richard Creagh-Osborne to say, "They're in for it."

David Sheahan required neither a gale warning nor the satellite picture to come to the same conclusion. Between 9:00 and 10:00 P.M., the wind built rapidly while the barometer plummeted, and by 11:00 P.M. *Grimalkin* was sailing at six knots under her tiny storm jib alone. Even a reefed mainsail was too much sail for this force 8 wind. Soon water started to come on deck while heavy rain drove down continuous and cold. The crew sealed off the cabin by placing the wooden slats, called washboards, in the companionway hatch, and rather than go below—where equipment, food, clothing, and bedding were flying everywhere as the boat rocked and rolled—all six men sat in the cockpit, their safety harnesses firmly hooked to the jackwires that Sheahan had so carefully installed. Gerry Winks steered *Grimalkin* on port tack out into the blackness of the Western Approaches, holding a course about 20 degrees off the rhumb line of 330 degrees to Fastnet Rock—and (though they did not know it) almost directly into the path of the dangerous quadrant of the depression. On starboard tack, heading south instead of northwest, they would have been steering away from the storm but also from Fastnet Rock. Storm or no, this crew would continue toward their objective until the boat ceased making headway.

Gerry Winks tired quickly. At 3:00 A.M., exhausted and shivering, he went below, where dry clothes and some food took the edge off his hypothermia, the dangerous loss of body heat that comes from prolonged exposure to cold air or water. At the helm, Nick Ward thought that the high, steep waves and powerful wind were part of a scene from a surrealistic film. No sail was possible, and they were unable to stay on course under bare poles. David Sheahan wondered out loud what they should do to try to cope with the seas ("these blocks of flats but three times as wide," Nick Ward called them). They eventually decided to run before it, effectively abandoning the race, with the wind and the waves on their stern, towing ropes overboard to try to keep their speed down. Yet even with six hundred feet of line dragging over the stern, *Grimalkin* was barely in control. She surfed wildly down the faces of the waves, like an elevator cut loose from its cable, and threatened to pitchpole, or somersault over her bow. She once accelerated to over twelve knots and, tilting forward until she was almost vertical, plunged down the face of a huge wave. Ward at the helm and Mike Doyle, sitting next to him, frantically looked to port and starboard for a flat spot to aim for, a landing field on which to level out, but all around was broiling white foam and ahead was a black wall—the back of the next wave rising out of the narrow trough. *Grimalkin* stuck her bow ten feet into the wall until her entire foredeck was buried three feet deep. The wall parted, and she shook off the tons of water and surfed off on another wave.

At least six times between 3:00 and 5:00 A.M. *Grimalkin* spun broadside to the faces of such waves and was caught under the curl and rolled until her mast was in the water. Each time, all six men were thrown out of the cockpit and left dangling by their safety harness tethers in the water or wrapped around the lifelines and backstay. A one-hundred-and-fifty-pound man generates a force of more than three thousand pounds when he is thrown twelve feet. The safety harnesses and jackwires withstood those loads, but the men themselves took a fearful beating.

On the fifth knockdown, Ward, who was still steering, was thrown entirely across the cockpit, over the lifelines, and into the water with his left leg tangled in the harness tether. As David and Matthew Sheahan dragged him aboard, Ward felt an unfamiliar sensation: his left leg hurt. He had not felt pain in that limb since the neurological attack eight years earlier. The leg, he decided, must have been broken when he hit the lifelines. He half sat, half lay in the cockpit while some of the men around him tensed themselves against the pounding waves and the driving wind simply to remain aboard a yacht that fell out from under them every time a wave passed.

David Sheahan slid open the companionway hatch and went below to radio for help. He reported their assumed position to *Morningtown*, the RORC's escort yacht, and he hoped that she would send it on to the coastguards. He soon reported to the men in the cockpit that spotter airplanes and helicopters were on the way. Mike Doyle attempted to light flares but he was unfamiliar with the ignition procedure and they merely fizzled into the sea.

Sheahan came back on deck just in time to be slung into the lifelines when *Grimalkin* was knocked flat once again. When the weight of her keel rolled her back upright, he lay in the cockpit, his head badly cut. The crew helped him below, where his son, Matthew, sprayed antiseptic into the wound. Seeing that the cabin was almost totally wrecked—the radios, chart table, engine housing, and companionway ladder were destroyed— they returned to the cockpit, which, though exposed, seemed safer than the shattered interior. In their inflated life jackets and safety harnesses, the six men huddled together for warmth and protection. Nick Ward's leg was causing him great pain, and Sheahan and Winks were dazed and frequently unconscious from their injuries and from hypothermia. Eventually, Winks was lowered to the cockpit sole where, at the others' feet, he had some degree of refuge.

The next knockdown was the worst. *Grimalkin* was capsized, rolled right over by a giant breaker. David Sheahan was trapped under the cockpit as the boat lay upside down. To free him, his crew cut his safety harness tether, and when the boat finally righted herself after half a minute or more, he drifted away helplessly, never to be seen again.

*Grimalkin* was dismasted in the capsize and her broken mast and rigging and boom now cluttered her deck. The five survivors dragged themselves back through the lifelines and rigging into the cockpit, where Nick Ward collapsed. Gerry Winks rolled, unconscious, on top of him.

Matthew Sheahan, Mike Doyle, and Dave Wheeler talked

over their situation and decided that *Grimalkin* was not safe. She was half full of water and wallowing dangerously, and in the gray morning light the seas seemed even more violent than they had before dawn. The skipper, Matthew's father, had been swept away to a sure death before their eyes, and their shipmates lay unconscious at their feet. They pulled the rolled-up, uninflated life raft out from its storage locker under the cockpit sole, pulled the line that triggered the $CO_2$ bottle, and watched the bundle of rubber raft inflate. A close look convinced them that if Winks and Ward were not dead, they soon would be, and that in either case they could never be dragged into the raft. Taking off their safety harnesses, they climbed gingerly into the life raft and pushed themselves away. The time was about 8:00 A.M.

The life raft turned out to be not much more reassuring than *Grimalkin* had been. Almost covered by the canopy, the three young men could barely see outside, and could only await help as they bailed out water thrown in by the waves. Yet rescue was only an hour in coming. A Sea King helicopter hovered overhead and dropped a wet-suited airman on a wire. As the airman in the water secured one man at a time in a harness, the winchman aloft let out slack in the wire and the pilot backed the helicopter downwind and rose well above the waves to stay away from the salt spray that might clog its turbines. When the airman in the water waved an "all ready," the pilot, flying blind because he could not see the raft, moved the machine slowly forward under instructions from the winchman in the cabin. The pilot elevated and dropped his helicopter in tune with the steep waves monotonously rolling down at him from the horizon, all the while following the winchman's instructions: "Six feet left, four forward . . . right over." The winchman pushed a button and *Grimalkin*'s survivors were fished out of the sea, one by one.

With all three yachtsmen on board, the Sea King set off in search of another life raft. When two survivors of a yacht named *Trophy* had been lifted aboard, the helicopter swung east. A few minutes later, the five exhausted, cold men were in the sick bay of the Royal Naval Air Station at Culdrose.

Neither *Grimalkin* nor the half-dead men in her cockpit received any grace after being abandoned by the others. She was rolled over once again. Nick Ward regained consciousness to find himself under water, his arms and legs tangled in stays and lines, his head being banged by the hull. He struggled to the surface, untangled himself, and painfully crawled up into the boat through a gap left in the lifelines by the destruction of two stanchions. From the cockpit, he saw Gerry Winks dragging overboard. Wrapping Winks's tether around a winch, he slowly winched his shipmate aboard. Winks was still alive. Using artificial respiration, Ward pumped water out of and breathed air into Winks's lungs, but the combined effects of the cold, exhaustion, and his own physical disability were fatal. Winks whispered, "If you see Margaret again, tell her I love her," and died.

Twenty-four-year-old Nick Ward was now alone with a dead man in a wrecked boat in a gale, without either a life raft or a functioning radio. His leg pained him and was possibly fractured and his back and shoulders ached from the beating that he had taken. His only course of action was to try to keep *Grimalkin* afloat and to hope for rescue. He staggered below, where everything was either shattered or afloat in the water. Even moving around in the cabin was dangerous, since the floorboards were floating, and loose food, broken crockery, and pieces of equipment continued to fly about as the boat rolled. David Sheahan had set aside four buckets for emergencies, but three had disappeared during the knockdowns and capsizes, leaving only the smallest for Ward to bail with. He established a schedule of one hour for bailing and thirty minutes off for rest in a wet and sometimes half-submerged bunk.

The bailing seemed to make no progress. He wondered if the transducer, the speedometer sensor projected through the hull, had fallen out. More likely, the gallons of water that had accumulated in shelves, drawers, sleeping bags, and clothing were now dripping down into the bilge.

*Grimalkin*, 8:00 P.M. Tuesday. *Royal Navy*

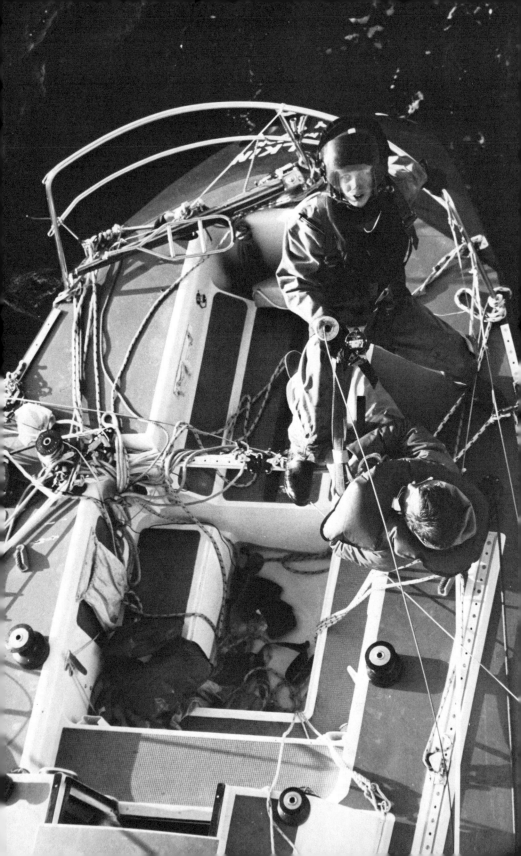

Whatever emotions he felt were focused on survival. His shock at Gerry Winks's death and the horror of realizing that he had been left behind by his shipmates were, he decided, subordinated to the energy he needed to survive. His great frustration was that the three who had abandoned *Grimalkin* were not on board to help him save her and, when the storm had subsided, to sail her to port under an emergency rig. Except for the small transducer hole, the hull seemed sound enough, and, Ward thought, there was a way to step a jury mast once the wind and sea calmed. But he could never do it alone. He held no personal grudge against the three. Rather he was angry at them for giving up on the boat.

To gain better access to the bilge, he ripped out two bunks and tossed sails and equipment forward into a pile. Rummaging through the debris in the lockers, he found some milk. He could not, however, locate his medicine, which he was meant to take every four hours. The doctors had said that he could do without it for perhaps a day, but no longer. He had last taken the medicine Monday night, nearly twelve hours before.

As Ward tried to keep to his schedule, estimating time because his watch had stopped, the sky cleared to an almost cloudless cold blue. The wind had shifted into the north-west and was chilling. It continued to blow very hard until midafternoon. The waves, which more than the wind had caused the capsizes, lengthened out. They were just as high as the night before, if not higher, but they were much less steep. Where they had broken and fallen on *Grimalkin* with fearful regularity, they now rolled under her relatively harmlessly. Nick Ward bailed and napped, bailed and napped all afternoon.

Sometime around 6:00 P.M., he heard an airplane pass close overhead. By the time he had scrambled into the cockpit, the

Airman Peter Harrison looks up at the helicopter from *Grimalkin*'s deck as Nick Ward waits to be lifted up. The well in the forward cockpit housed the life raft, which was inflated some twelve hours earlier by the three men who abandoned the boat, leaving Ward and Gerry Winks. The large snaphooks in the bottom right-hand corner are at the ends of the tethers of two safety harnesses and are hooked to a jackwire running from the cockpit to the bow. The lifelines have been cut by the broken mast. *Royal Navy*

plane had disappeared. To avoid a recurrence of that disappointment, he remained in the cockpit, securing his weary, hurting body next to Gerry Winks's corpse with his safety harness and the mainsheet.

Another yacht soon appeared out of the waves. Ward was able to attract her attention with blasts on a foghorn. Although they had no transmitter, her crew fired off several flares that attracted the attention of a third yacht, which radioed a request for assistance. As dusk began to fall over the Western Approaches, Nick Ward saw a helicopter come at him rapidly from the east. The helicopter swung up and hovered forty feet overhead, and a man dropped quickly from the door on its right side onto the dismasted *Grimalkin*'s deck. Weeping with relief, Ward helped the airman secure Wink's body to the harness. After the corpse was hauled into the helicopter, the harness dropped down again. Talking barely coherently, Ward told the airman to wait. "I must get my clothes from below," he said. But the airman told him it was too late, that *Grimalkin* was sinking. As they were hauled through the air to the helicopter, Nick Ward looked down at the now truly abandoned sloop and quietly thanked her for providing refuge. He also thought how sad it was that nobody had stayed behind to help him keep her afloat.

# 3 TOSCANA: To the Western Approaches

LONGER FOREKNOWLEDGE of the approach of Low Y probably would not have decreased the havoc caused by the storm in the Western Approaches. We in *Toscana*, an American forty-eight-foot sloop whose home port was Westport, Connecticut, had come too far to drop out of this Fastnet race simply because of a few warnings about bad weather, and I don't believe that David Sheahan would have stopped racing before the conditions actually deteriorated to the point where survival was the overriding consideration. Of the two dozen or so other boats in the Fastnet fleet that lost men overboard, suffered incapacitating damage, or were abandoned by their crews, perhaps one or two—but no more—might have run for shelter if the "Fastnet, force 10" warning had been made during the BBC Radio 4 shipping bulletin early on Monday morning. The challenge of sailing through rough weather is indisputably one of the attractions of ocean racing. Whether or not the challenge has been compromised by the death and destruction that occurred in the Fastnet race gale, it was pure and golden to the men and women who started the race at Cowes on August 11, 1979.

This summer gale, packing all the violence of a midwinter North Atlantic storm, could not have appeared at a more unlucky moment. If it had arrived a day earlier, most of the boats would have been within sight of the safe harbors indenting the English Channel, where they might have found shelter before the wind abated sufficiently for them to continue racing. And twelve or fifteen hours later, the smaller, more vulnerable boats would have

---

*Toscana* **during the Cowes Week force 9 gale on Thursday, August 9. Forty-eight feet in length, she was designed by Sparkman and Stephens, New York, and built in Finland by Nautor. She was raced across the Atlantic in July 1979 by her owner, Eric Swenson, for Cowes Week and the Fastnet race. Here, she is carrying her storm spinnaker and double-reefed mainsail.** *Louis Kruk*

been within easy reach of the safe ports along the south-east coast of Ireland.

Attacked by surprise, at night, halfway between England and Ireland, most of the fleet had to rely only on seamanship and luck. For many crews, neither was sufficient. At its worst, the gale was fiercer than any storm ever experienced by the overwhelming majority of the sailors caught in it.

Since it was first sailed in 1925, the Fastnet race has been one of the major goals of racing yachtsmen throughout the world. Other ocean races are longer (transatlantic and Honolulu races run more than two thousand miles) or, if the same length, cover more blue water (unlike the Fastnet, which runs along a coast for almost half its length, the Bermuda race is across part of an open ocean), but the Fastnet race is the international standard of ocean yacht racing. Alfred F. Loomis, historian of the sport, called the Fastnet "the Grand National of ocean racing." That Loomis, an American, referred to an English and not an American horse race is no coincidence. Until quite recently in the United States, yachting has been the preserve of white Anglo-Saxon Protestants who, like Loomis, tend to evaluate their institutions by English standards.

I myself am almost purely WASP, despite my French name (and it is probably Huguenot, anyway). A French commissary worker helping out during the American Revolution left the name in Newport, Rhode Island, when he sailed home in 1783. His only American son, Lewis, was a successful Newport publisher until he invested in merchant ships. They were soon unlucky in meeting their schedules, and Lewis, finding himself bankrupt at age thirty-seven, slit his throat with a shoemaker's knife. One of Lewis's sons, William, "followed sea," according to a nephew. Nothing else is known of sailor William. Another son, John, became the foreman of the printing department of the *Boston Daily Advertiser*. Much is known of John. The family avoided the sea for three generations until my father became interested in sailboat racing and won junior and intercollegiate championships in the thirties. He passed that interest and some of his skill on to me. Though he never sailed in a Fastnet race,

he had raced in Scotland and our library was full of British sailing books—in brief, although I challenged most WASP princi-
ples, I never questioned the dogma that yachting was best conducted in waters off the British Isles, and that ocean racing
achieved its greatest fulfillment near Fastnet Rock.

Races across the Atlantic and to Bermuda, Nassau, Spain,
and Baja California, races around the Florida Keys and the
length of two Great Lakes, races up the east coast and down the
west coast all passed, but the Fastnet remained the gleam in
my eye. When I was thirty-five, Eric Swenson (another WASP)
asked me to sail with him in 1979 on a transatlantic race to
Ireland, a short Irish cruise, and then the Cowes Week series of
five races off the Isle of Wight, followed by the Fastnet race. I
hadn't the time for both parts of the schedule. Despite my affection for long offshore passages, in which the simple man-in-
nature pleasures of living aboard are stretched out for weeks on
end, I told Eric that I would be there for Cowes Week and, of
course, the Fastnet.

"Impressive Cowes Week Had Its Dramas," ran a headline
in the *Isle of Wight County Press* on the eve of the start of the
Fastnet race. It was an understatement. Over eight hundred
boats raced daily off a single starting line, dodging press boats,
the Royal Yacht *Britannia*, ferries, and, sometimes, each other.
One sailor broke his arm when a Brazilian boat rammed an
Australian boat. Another Brazilian boat was holed and almost
sunk by an Argentinian boat. A Belgian skipper died of a heart
attack during one race, and, on another day, a Belgian crew
member was dragged across a deck by a runaway sheet and
knocked unconscious. Former prime minister Edward Heath's
*Morning Cloud* lost her rudder during the overnight Channel
race and was later badly gouged by vandals while she sat at her
mooring. In one race in heavy winds, two sailors on different
boats were badly injured in the head by flying booms. One, a
Japanese sailor, was carried off his boat at the end of the race,
but the wound to an Englishman was so severe that he was
immediately taken from his boat in a photographer's rubber
dinghy, from which he was hoisted by an air-sea rescue heli-

copter and taken to a hospital. And during the last race of Cowes Week, sailed in a force 8 to force 9 gale, we in *Toscana* picked up a man in mid-Solent from his capsized powerboat.

Whether random accidents or incidents in a pattern of omens, these events did not affect the start of the Fastnet race. A fleet of 303 yachts, the largest ever to enter the race, was sent off by the Royal Yacht Squadron's cannon at ten-minute intervals between 1:30 and 2:30 P.M. Saturday, August 11. There were six divisions, based on size of boat. The largest entrant was *Kialoa*, John Kilroy's seventy-nine-foot sloop from Los Angeles, California. The smallest were two twenty-eight-footers, *Billy Bones*, owned by two French sailors named Boudet and Seuly, and *Arkadina*, owned by an Englishman named A.J. Boutle. The average boat was thirty-eight feet, two inches long and probably weighed about fifteen thousand pounds. Twenty-two countries were represented, among them most of the major European, North and South American, and Australasian nations. Nineteen of those countries had entered teams in the competition for the Admiral's Cup, considered by ocean-racing sailors to be their sport's unofficial world championship. Almost every one of the fifty-seven Admiral's Cuppers had been built within the previous eight months and was a highly refined, relatively lightweight, single-purpose racing boat. Going into the Fastnet race, Ireland was leading the Cup series with the United States, Australia, and Hong Kong (many of whose sailors were Englishmen with dual citizenship) trailing in that order. According to the fleet roster circulated before the start by the Royal Ocean Racing Club, 165 entrants were British, 55 were French, 16 were Irish, and 12 were American. The only entry requirements were that the boats have an International Offshore Rule rating, used for comparing boats of different sizes and characteristics against each other, of at least 20.1 feet and that they carry certain

---

**Strong winds during Cowes Week had many of the racing boats out of control, especially on downwind legs under the press of large spinnakers. Here, the Polish Admiral's Cupper *Nauticus* broaches to windward in a force 6 (twenty-two- to twenty-seven-knot) breeze.** *William Payne*

A navy helicopter crew during the rescue of Richard Bagnall during Cowes Week.
Bagnall, whose skull had been fractured by the boom of his Irish-owned yacht, is
hoisted aloft while an airman stems the flow of blood. Bagnall was in a hospital within half
an hour after his serious injury. *William Payne photographs*

required safety equipment, including flares, life jackets, man-overboard floats, lights, a radio receiver, and a life raft. Virtually any cruising sailboat larger than twenty-eight feet might have qualified to sail in the race.

Weather forecasts issued at Cowes on the eve and day of the start anticipated moderate to fresh winds over the succeeding three days, with a likelihood of strong winds by Tuesday. No boat or crew should have had any difficulty with those conditions, and, given the forecasters' reputation for occasional exaggeration, this forecast should not have deterred anybody from starting the race. However, it was (and still is) fair to assume that any crew that enters a six-hundred-mile race off the English coast is prepared for bad weather. Although recent Fastnet races had been sailed in light winds, the race has been considered a rough one from its genesis, in 1925.

Ocean racing—competition between sailing yachts over distances greater than two hundred miles—has been a popular sport only since the mid-1920s. Developing first in the United States, with long races across the Atlantic, to Hawaii, and on the Great Lakes, the sport as we know it today began with the 1923 race from New London, Connecticut, to Bermuda. Intrigued by the novel idea of racing long distances in small boats, English yachtsmen set about to found their own contest. The first Fastnet race was sailed in 1925, though not to unanimous approval. Many Englishmen thought their waters too dangerous for the requirements of racing, one of which is that the crew carries on in rough weather even to the point of risking damage to the boat. An influential critic was a yacht designer, Claud Worth, who counseled caution. A privately arranged race between two owners would be one thing, he wrote in the sporting magazine *The Field,* "but a public race might very well include some owners whose keenness is greater than their experience. If the weather should be bad, so long as there is a head wind they would probably come to no harm, for a good boat and sound gear will generally stand as much driving as the crew can put up with. But when running before anything approaching a gale of wind and a big sea in open water, conditions are very deceptive. It requires much judgment to know whether a following sea has reached the dangerous stage. I have more than once been compelled very reluctantly to heave-to and watch a fair wind running to waste, and have soon after had reason to be very thankful that I was safely hove-to in good time.

"But if one had been racing one would probably have been tempted to carry on, knowing that some other competitor might take the risk. These conditions might not occur once in a dozen races, but the magnitude of possible disaster should be taken into account."

Worth knew his English weather. During the gale-torn 1931 race Colonel C. H. Hudson was swept overboard and lost from the fifty-one-foot cutter *Maitenes II*, of which he was a part owner. Yet Worth's worries did not apply in this case. *Maitenes II* was hove-to, her crew deciding not to risk running before a force 9 westerly gale, and Hudson apparently did not observe the old rule of keeping one hand for oneself and one hand for the ship. (This incident apparently was overlooked in 1979 when the press and the Royal Ocean Racing Club reported that the only prior fatality in the fifty-four years and twenty-eight runnings of the Fastnet race was a man who died of a heart attack in 1977.)

The 1957 race was the roughest Fastnet race before 1979. That gale was anticipated, however. In his book *Yacht and Sea*, the Swedish yacht designer Gustav Plym described an abrupt conversation he had with the Royal Ocean Racing Club's commodore before the start. "Any last-minute orders?" Plym asked. "None whatever," answered the commodore. "There is a gale warning, but there is no real vice in it. Good luck."

The 1957 race started in a Channel gale that eventually built to force 9, and twenty-nine of the forty-one starters dropped out before reaching Land's End. The remainder of the race was relatively easy. On board Plym's *Elseli IV*, "our experience gave us strength. . . . There was no thought of giving up—at least not in the skipper's mind, and whatever the crew may have thought they were too well disciplined to whisper a word about it." Plym described "high-breaking mountains of water" and "the screaming sound in the rigging" that was like "the shriek of a woman in despair." The motion of the boat was so wild, he wrote, that sleep was impossible and "it was a relief to be called on deck after a couple of hours." Another of the twelve finishers was a badly leaking American yawl, *Carina*, whose owner, Richard S. Nye, said to his crew as she crossed the finish line at Plymouth, "All right, boys, we're over now. Let her sink." (Uttered within two miles of one of Britain's largest commercial ports, this jest has since been assigned the aura of gospel instruction by the few true masochists who sail.) *Carina* had fallen off a wave, much the way a man might lose his footing on a log that rolls out from under him, and the impact of the nineteen-ton yacht dropping several feet had cracked some of her frames. *Carina* won the race, as she had in 1955. American yachts have won eight of the twenty-eight Fastnet races.

"The seas were positively tumultuous," K. Adlard Coles wrote of the 1957 gale in his book *Heavy Weather Sailing*, a study of bad storms that he and other racing sailors had survived. When I first read this book, I had nightmares about huge breakers, and survivors of the 1979 Fastnet were describing the waves they had encountered as being "just like those frightening pictures in Coles."

We were an experienced crew in *Toscana*, which had just sailed a three-thousand-mile transatlantic race. Eric Swenson, her skipper and one watch captain, had raced her and his other boats in four Bermuda races, and I, the other watch captain, had covered over thirty thousand miles offshore in several boats. The navigator, Captain John Coote, Royal Navy (Retired), had raced in twelve Fastnets and several Bermuda and Australian races. We may have been one of the few boats in the race to have women standing watches. If she is quick and knowledgeable, a woman can be as helpful on deck as any man, although she may not be as strong. Susan Noyes had sailed all her life, and Sherry Jagerson had raced to Bermuda and to Ireland in *Toscana*. The least experienced racing sailor on board was Stuart Woods, an American writer, but even he had offshore experience, having sailed in a single-handed transatlantic race. The boat herself was well designed and stoutly built for offshore sailing. One of a type called the Swan 47, *Toscana* was designed by the New York firm of Sparkman and Stephens and strongly built of fiberglass by a Finnish yard called Nautor. Her oversized rigging made the masts on the Admiral's Cup boats seem like fishing rods.

In many ways, *Toscana* represented the old traditions of ocean racing, once a gentleman's sport in which a few hundred friends and acquaintances cruised in company with and raced against one another, year in and year out, in boats designed to go to sea. Over the previous half-dozen years, a group of young yacht designers, sailmakers, and builders had developed and crewed in a new breed of sophisticated and extremely fast boats for a generation of highly competitive owners. At the very top level of racing, the Admiral's Cup fleet, these owners bought and sold boats annually in order to keep up with developments in design and construction. In this nautical equivalent of Grand Prix automobile racing, the boats were shipped from country to country for a handful of important regattas. While there was no professionalism in the sport in the sense that winners receive cash prizes, there was a kind of semiprofessionalism in which boat and equipment manufacturers stood to gain in the long run when they and their products helped Grand Prix yachts win important races and regattas. The boats usually were financed by wealthy men whose fortunes derived from real estate, manufacturing, and other entrepreneurial enterprises. Most of them sailed in their boats, sometimes in command and sometimes as a privileged crew member; a few, like owners of race horses, were content to stay ashore. Built in some cases with experimental materials, rigged with the most sophisticated equipment, and nurtured with hundreds of thousands of dollars, these yachts were the Ferraris of the sport.

By comparison, *Toscana* was a Mercedes-Benz. Her owner, who had raced production sports cars, had no desire to own one of those exotic boats. Although fast, many of the new racing machines were difficult to steer and often very uncomfortable. Excess weight was eliminated with passion: their galleys were skimpy, their toilets were separated from the living areas by a curtain (if at all), and their interiors had all the charm of the in-

*Above, left: Siska*, a seventy-seven-footer that was shipped to England by her Australian owner, slams through a force 9 (forty-one- to forty-seven-knot) gale two days before the Fastnet race start under triple-reefed mainsail and forestaysail, the rig carried by *Toscana* during the worst part of the Fastnet gale. *Alastair Black*

*Above, right:* Their names inspired by a poem by William Butler Yeats, *Golden Apple of the Sun* (IR 206) and *Silver Apple of the Moon* both suffered broken rudders in the Fastnet race. *Golden Apple*'s crew abandoned their yacht for a life raft, which was almost swamped, in order to be picked up by a helicopter. *Barry Pickthall*

The American forty-five-foot Admiral's Cup boat *Williwaw* finishes a Cowes Week race to a cloud of cannon smoke from the Royal Yacht Squadron. Like most ocean racers, she has a flush deck and is arranged more for crew efficiency than for cruising comfort. *Williwaw* finished the Fastnet race after being knocked down several times. *William Payne*

side of an airplane's wing, with strengthening struts and structural members jutting into the bunks and living areas. Eric Swenson liked his comfort, and his *Toscana* had a freezer in the galley, hot and cold running water, two enclosed toilets with showers, six built-in bunks (one a double berth), several lockers for hanging clothes, and enough teak and other hardwoods laid over the fiberglass to build a small, elegant house. Hanging on her stern was a swimming ladder, which Swenson justified by claiming that it was an excellent means for recovering men who had gone overboard, but which many Grand Prix skippers would have thrown right off the boat as excess weight. (Swenson might not have had a Grand Prix skipper of such seriousness on board to begin with; while he respected their talents and dedication, he felt that theirs was a different type of sport from his.)

After the start, we cleared the Needles, at the western entrance to the Solent, and sailed out into the English Channel in a wind that died to force 3. It was from the southwest, dead ahead, and we beat to windward at six to seven knots, choosing the tack that would take us closest to our objective, a point 180 miles away called the Lizard. We alternated watches four hours on, four hours off between 7:00 P.M. and 7:00 A.M. and at six-hour intervals during the day. Francie McBride, the pretty, chatty Irish cook, served up meals at the watch changes, and once expressed chagrin when she realized that she had not brought the correct type of cream for a complicated desert pudding. My watch was four—John Ruch, Susan Noyes, Nick Noyes, and myself (the Noyeses are unrelated)—and John Coote volunteered to come on deck to steer while we made sail changes, which was often.

People who say that ocean racing is boring have never worked hard at it. Racing rules, modern technology, and the boat owner's money have provided large numbers of sails, each of which has a specialized purpose and can be readily substituted for another sail as the wind lightens, strengthens, or shifts in direction. *Toscana* carried eighteen sails in bins in the forwardmost of her three cabins, on the sole (the floor) of the main cabin, and in a bin in the after cabin. Nine of these sails were

**Life aboard an ocean racer in moderate winds: part of the crew of** *Kialoa,* **an American seventy-nine-footer, eats during a race. At the head of the table is the owner, John Kilroy.** *Louis Kruk*

jibs that we set off the headstay, which leads from the top of the mast to the bow. Each jib was designed to be used in a particular wind strength or direction, and if either changed by as little as a couple of knots or five degrees, the crew would change to another jib. The sails were known by numbers or by names: the number 1 (of which we had two) was the largest, number 2 the next largest, and so on down to the number 4; the drifter was used in very light winds, the reaching jib was used only when sailing across the wind (whereas the numbered sails might be used either when reaching or when beating into the wind), the blooper, or big boy, was set when running, and the tiny storm jib, smaller even than the number 4, was reserved for the very rare force 9 or stronger gale. We could change jibs quickly since *Toscana* was equipped with a twin-slotted plastic foil that was secured over the headstay. The boltropes on the luff, or forward edge, of the jibs were fed into the slots as the halyard was hoisted. To change sails, we hoisted the new sail in the free slot on another halyard and then pulled the old sail down. In theory this worked well; in practice it jammed regularly.

Besides the nine jibs, we also could choose from among three staysails, which were set either free or on the forestay, which ran from two-thirds of the way up the mast to a point on the deck six feet behind the bow. These relatively small sails generally improved the boat's speed when reaching.

In addition, *Toscana* carried four spinnakers of various weights and sizes. These huge multicolored nylon sails were set when we reached across the wind or ran before it. The smallest spinnaker was used in strong winds when we thought we might be overpowered with the largest one set. Finally, we had aboard a spare mainsail and a storm trysail, a very small mainsail set, as the name implies, in bad gales. Neither the spare mainsail nor the trysail was required by the rules that applied in the Fastnet race, but like all the other boats, we were obligated to carry the storm jib.

The permanently set mainsail was equipped with three reefs, which we could use to change the sail's shape or to decrease the square footage of sail exposed to the wind as the breeze strengthened. With the third reef tied in, the sail was approximately 60 percent its maximum, unreefed size. With three reefs in the mainsail and the storm jib or forestaysail set, we would carry about one-third the square footage of Dacron that would be up with the full mainsail and number-1 jib hoisted.

Each sail was trimmed with at least one sheet (spinnakers have two sheets) with which we could establish the optimum shape for a given wind strength and direction. We could also alter sail shape by adjusting halyard tension with powerful stainless-steel winches and by changing the bend of the mast and the altitude of the boom with hydraulic pumps on the backstay and the boom vang. At any moment, we could make as many as eight adjustments, most of them synergetic—changing one control often required alterations in two or three others. I enjoyed fooling around with all this gear and could sail an entire four-hour watch at night or a six-hour watch during the day without once sitting still. Sometimes I should have sat still and left things alone. Not only did all this nervous energy drive my watchmates crazy, but impatient sail trimming was as likely to slow a boat down as it was to speed her up.

We measured *Toscana*'s ability to use the wind best in a variety of ways. If a boat of about her size were alongside, we could compare speeds by sight. If competitors were out of sight, we evaluated our performance by "feel"—the tug of the steering wheel and the boat's motion through the waves—and with the help of a veritable dashboard of instruments directly in front of the helmsman. From left to right, there were an anemometer for wind speed, zero to sixty knots; an apparent wind indicator that showed the direction of the wind relative to our heading; a speedometer, which flashed out digital displays of our speed through the water to a one-hundredth of a knot; and a depth sounder, which indicated the amount of water beneath the hull. Steering by these dials and by the compass, mounted in the binnacle squarely in front of the wheel, was a bit like driving a car at

OVERLEAF: The wind and boat speed, wind direction, and other instruments in *Kialoa* were duplicated in most Fastnet race entries. *Louis Kruk*

high speed in heavy traffic. The helmsman's eyes constantly flickered from one indicator to the other as he tried to sail the course at the highest speed, and with the corner of his eye he kept a watch for waves, which, if they were from astern, might increase our speed, or, if from ahead, could slow us. At night the helmsman could not see much beyond the dials, which were lit with faint white or red lights, and had to anticipate waves through the motion of the boat.

As we beat toward the Lizard, we changed sails with almost every alteration in wind strength. The crew carefully folded the jib that had been doused, bagged it in a blue sack, and dropped it below through the forward hatch. Sometimes as soon as we had changed sails, the wind died or increased to the point where we had to change right back. Somebody would have to go below and push the heavy, bulky sail up through the hatch, where another person lugged it on deck.

Most if not all of our competitors had at least the same number of sails and instruments and were racing as aggressively as we were in *Toscana*. From time to time, another boat would sail across our bow or wake. Sometimes she was smaller than *Toscana*—in light winds, little boats can sail as fast as big boats—sometimes she was a bit larger. The second day, Sunday the twelfth, a freighter steamed out of the fog at ten knots only a couple of hundred yards ahead. We sailed to within a quarter mile of the Eddystone Light with no evidence of the lighthouse's existence other than its mournful horn and its bright rotating light two hundred feet up. Fog is caused by a mixing of cool water and warm damp air. In some areas, fog comes before wind; in other areas, it may come before bad weather. I did not know enough about the English Channel to be certain just what this fog meant, but I was not happy to be in it in a shipping lane.

Late that night, we bore off around the Lizard, set the reaching jib, and headed toward the Runnelstone buoy, just off Land's End. When our watch was relieved by Eric's at 11:00 P.M., *Toscana* was reaching at nine knots. When we returned to deck at 3:00 A.M., for the dawn watch, we were still sailing fast. The dawn watch is my favorite time of day offshore. The crew on deck has a ringside seat for the sun's early pyrotechnics, which, in the unpolluted air over the sea, are quick and orange, unlike the slow red dawns over land. The sun quickly warms fingers that have been chilled during the darkest, coldest hour of night that comes just before dawn. What appeals to me most about watching the sun rise at sea is the chiaroscuro effect of the new light softening the hard edges of objects and people in those last minutes of blackness.

Dawn often brings a drop in the wind. That morning, the breeze quickly died from a solid fifteen knots to a calm, and when members of Eric's watch poked their heads up through the hatch at 7:00 A.M. to relieve us, we were struggling to inch the boat's speedometer up over one knot. *Toscana* and the dozen or so boats around her were inscribing slow circles over the groundswell rolling in from the south-west. For the first time since the race started forty-two hours earlier, we were out of wind. We were at sea, in the Western Approaches.

I dozed over breakfast—we had worked hard on deck for eight of the ten hours of darkness. When I finished that huge English breakfast, I thanked the cook and went aft to the owner's cabin. Susan, Nick, and John Slept in bunks in the main cabin, but following tradition, the watch captains and the navigator slept aft, in the owner's cabin that was almost under the cockpit and, therefore, most directly accessible to any deck crew who needed advice. By sheerest coincidence, bunks toward the stern of a yacht are more stable (hence easier to sleep in) than those farther forward. Eric and I traded off in one bunk. John Coote did not stand watch, so he had the starboard bunk in perpetuity, although he rarely used it and spent most of his time in the seat at the navigator's table, on the starboard side of the main cabin across from the galley. There, he operated the radio direction finder, the only electronic navigation tool we were allowed to use, and plotted our positions and courses. He also chatted with Francie, patiently answered the barrage of questions that came from the nine men and women standing watches ("Where are we? How many miles to the Rock? What's the weather forecast?"), and leaned his considerable bulk against the cabin side for cat naps. When the BBC shipping bulletins were about due, he took his portable radio aft and into his bunk, where he curled up and, in quiet privacy, dozed through the farm news until the weather forecasts came on.

I slept soundly for five hours that morning. When awakened for lunch, I dressed and went into the main cabin. A wet, badly torn spinnaker lay at the foot of the companionway and we were heeled well over to starboard. Coote filled me in on the details: the wind had finally filled in from the north-east ("A strange direction, don't you think?") and Eric's watch had set the spinnaker. Later, the wind strengthened and veered through east to south. While they were dousing the spinnaker, the other watch witnessed the unhappy spectacle of the cloth being blown by a hard puff right out of the tapes that defined its edges. They retrieved the fragments and threw them below.

After lunch, I briefly went on deck to sniff the weather. It was chilly and spray was in the air. Back below into the warm dry cabin, I alerted my watchmates to the cold and went aft to dress in four layers—long underwear, heavy shirt, sweater, and foul-weather gear.

An hour into our watch, at 2:00 P.M., Coote slid open the cover over the after companionway, poked his head up, and said, "South-west force 4 to 5, veering to west force 6 to 7. Fastnet Rock reports force 6 south-west." He looked absently at the steering wheel for a moment, then pulled his head below under the closing cover. That summary of the BBC's 1:55 shipping bulletin came as no surprise. We were reaching at eight and a half knots in about twenty-five knots of wind on the anemometer. Since about four knots of the wind's force was apparent wind created by Toscana's motion, we already had the force 5. The sky to the west was bifurcated. To the south-west, off our port bow, there were high white cirrus clouds. To the north-west, off our starboard bow, there were darker altocumulus "mackerel scales." I remembered the old seamen's warning: "Mackerel scales, furl your sails." Which was more correct, the forecast or the clouds with their suggestion of harsher weather?

We reached all afternoon, always on the verge of reefing.

The wind stayed between twenty and twenty-five knots and the boat was handling well. At six o'clock, I went below to warm my hands and hear Coote's summary of the 5:50 BBC shipping bulletin. The prediction continued to be for no worse than force 6, but the wind was expected to veer to north-west. There was a chance of a force 8 gale at Fastnet Rock, now ninety miles to the north-west. I tapped the barometer. Since the start, it had fallen from 1020 millibars (30.1 inches) to 1010 millibars (29.8 inches), still comparatively high. The BBC reported that it was at 1005 millibars (29.7 inches) and dropping slowly at Valentia Island, forty-six miles north-west of Fastnet Rock. Despite the barious omens of accidents, injuries, fog, calm, and clouds, the forecast and the barometer gave us little reason to worry about storms— although we could expect a force 8 near the Rock when we arrived there in ten hours, at 4:00 A.M. Tuesday morning.

An hour later, the watch changed in the middle of a rain squall, and, grateful for the timing, we went below to a beef curry dinner and a bottle of red wine. We were down to our last few bottles, which were fine sleeping aids for the off-going watches. The great mystery on board concerned the whereabouts of a case of white wine, which somebody claimed to have brought aboard at Cowes and which had somehow disappeared. Losing a case of wine in a forty-eight-foot boat would appear to be impossible, but apparently it had happened, and Coote, whose wine it was, spent his spare minutes ransacking lockers. If this story had not been true, it might have been invented by somebody trying to inject levity into the otherwise serious business of taking a boat offshore. (The wine was never found.) After dinner, I went aft into the owner's cabin, shed my four layers of clothes, and climbed into the cocoonlike bunk to snuggle under a blanket against the blue canvas lee cloth. This restrained me from rolling out of the bunk and down to the cabin sole.

I slept well for over two hours. When I first sailed offshore, in my late teens, I never had a problem with sleep, but I never had any responsibility either. Captaining a watch may have put me in closer tune with the boat: when she rests, I rest; when she works, I work. *Toscana* must have sailed along restfully for those

two hours ("snoring along on an easy reach" is how Alfred
Loomis aptly described such a sail), for I slept comfortably until
awakened by a new motion. She was pitching and rolling wildly.
Overhead, voices shouted, "Ten knots! Ten-point-*two! Ten-
point-two-five knots!!"*

I reached into the bin beside my head for my glasses and put
them on and crawled out of the cocoon. My left shoulder against
the lockers on the port side of the cabin—the boat was heeling at
least thirty degrees—I walked in my underwear through the
door to the main cabin, grabbing the support bar in front of the
stove. Downhill, John Coote dozed in the navigator's seat. In a
moment, his eyes opened and he said, as though continuing a
conversation, "They are doing over ten knots with the number 3
and one reef in the main. They should have the second reef in."

I swung downhill using the wooden companionway ladder as
a support, coming to a stop against the end of the navigator's
table. The built-in clock read 10:20. Forty minutes to the change
of watch. Coote pointed with a pencil to an encircled "X" on the
chart. About fifty miles to the Rock.

"How do we rig the third reef?" he asked gloomily.

"We get the bravest, tallest man on the boat to stand on the
boom and pass the free reefing line through the leech cringle." I
did not relish this chore. The week before, during Cowes Week,
booms had laid open two heads; six months earlier, a boom had
crushed the skull of a man during a race off Florida; a year ago,
my closest friend had twice been knocked into hospital
emergency rooms by flying booms. Booms are not to be messed
with in rough weather.

I looked around the cabin. My three watchmates and the
cook were asleep in the bunks. The lee cloths secured to the two
uphill bunks bulged around heads, buttocks, and shoulders. The
two in the downhill bunks were sleeping more on lockers and
the side of the hull than they were on their mattresses. I
climbed up to the galley, turned on the propane gas valves, lit a
burner, and put the pot over the flame. I slid back aft to dress:
damp long underwear, damp wool socks, damp green turtleneck
jersey, damp gray wool sweater, my last dry corduroy trousers,

fingerless leather gloves (my hands would soften in the spray). I pulled my foul-weather gear out of a locker and tugged on the suspendered yellow pants, which covered me from insteps to armpits. With a clownish balancing act, hopping on one foot, I shoved my feet into the damp yellow boots.

I inched forward again to the galley, with new security on the nonskid soles of the boots, and spooned instant coffee and condiments into four mugs: black for Nick, powdered milk and sugar for Susan and John, powdered milk for me. Leaving the other three mugs lying against a low rail around a shelf, I put my mug in one of the two stainless-steel sinks, turned off the gas, picked up the pot, and very carefully poured boiling water into the mug. As I picked it up and sipped at the coffee, I reflected on how calm I felt, how cautiously and purposefully I seemed to be moving. At any other time, I would have held the mug with one hand while trying to pour the water with the other. Inevitably, in the bouncing and heaving of the boat, my arm would have lurched and a drop or two would have spilled and scalded my hand. Had I slept that well? Was I anticipating something?

I had felt and moved this way once before, while preparing to parachute out of a U.S. Army troop plane. Then I had carefully put on my field gear and parachute, had moved cautiously through the inspections and into the plane, had sat quietly as the plane took off and circled over the drop zone, and had, with a keen sensitivity to my hands, stood up, hooked my harness to the static line, and shuffled to the door to jump, slow motion it seemed, into the air eighteen hundred feet above red Georgia soil.

# 4  TOSCANA: Battle Scene

WATER DRIPPING FROM her frizzy hair, Sherry Jagerson came below at 10:40 to awaken the new watch. The blackness and the roar of waves and wind burst through the open hatch into the sanctuary of the dimly lit cabin. As my watchmates rolled out of their bunks, I poured water and handed them their coffee. "You're already up?" John Ruch asked sleepily.

I drank my coffee carefully, put the mug in the sink, and went aft once again and pulled on my blue parka, insulated with foam to keep me afloat if I went overboard, and a brown wool hat. Leaning against a locker, I untangled the nylon straps of the safety harness and put it on. At the end of the six-foot-long tether was a heavy stainless-steel mountain climber's hook, which I snapped into the buckle to keep the tether from tangling in my legs. Moving stiffly in the six layers of clothing and the harness, I walked forward, climbed up the companionway ladder, pulled back the heavy Plexiglas hatch cover, and stuck my head up into the gale.

Sliding out of the hatch on my belly, I grabbed the safety line rigged between the companionway and the cockpit with one hand and reached behind me with the other to pull the hatch cover securely shut. I duck-walked aft, looking downwind to keep spray off my face, and, when I reached the cockpit, found a spot of bench to sit on among the four dark figures that braced themselves against the wind and the mad jerking of the boat. I hooked my safety harness to the line and concentrated on the rows of white-capped waves that marched downwind from us. When my eyes were adjusted to the dark and my internal

PRECEDING PHOTOGRAPH: Seas break on Fastnet Rock at midday on Tuesday, August 14. The gale is slowly moderating, but the seas are still heavy. Later, the lighthouse keepers washed thick salt layers off the lantern. *Irish Times*

rhythms were more or less in synchrony with *Toscana*'s lurches, I turned and studied the glowing instrument dials: wind speed—thirty-five, forty, thirty-seven knots; relative wind angle—ninety, one hundred, ninety degrees; boat speed— (dropping as we went up a wave) 9.95, 9.82, 9.50, 9.3, (increasing down a wave) 9.46, 9.70, 10.01, 10.25.

I turned the other way and wiped the spray off my glasses with my fingers. At the helm was Dale Cheek, an Oklahoman and former skipper of a Greek charter yacht who had turned up at the dock in Cowes one day looking for a crew berth. Fortunately for us, we took him, and Eric asked him along for the Fastnet race. Dale was struggling with the wheel. The king spoke, marked with a bit of line, stands vertical when the rudder is centered. Now it was horizontal, so the rudder below us was pushing thousands of pounds of water to one side, risking damage (perhaps), slowing us down (probably), and hindering Dale from steering the course (certainly).

"Eric, we should shorten down," I said.

"I agree," he said. "This blow just came up. We put up the number 3 only an hour ago."

"Another reef and the number-4 jib?" I asked.

"I think the forestaysail."

"Will it be enough sail to get us around the Rock? We'll have to tack, and the waves must be breaking there."

"That's five hours away," Swenson said. "Look how fast this is building."

We stared at the anemometer. The pointer now was between forty and forty-five knots. I looked around. Each of my watchmates was on deck, so we had nine pairs of hands. Eric took the helm.

"Okay," I said loudly. "First let's get the second reef in, next let's set the staysail, then let's douse the number 3."

Nobody budged. A large wave broke on deck and spray flew over us and halfway up the mainsail. Blobs of phosphorus, nature's light show, glowed for a few seconds on the sail and our foul-weather gear before sliding off and running out the cockpit drains.

I unhooked my harness, slid to leeward under the safety line, and grabbed an end of a spare jib sheet that lay on the leeward seat. I walked forward with the end along the starboard deck, leaning thirty degrees to port to stay upright and bracing myself against the boom with my left hand. Halfway forward, I leaned down and snapped the harness hook onto the jackwire that ran along the deck, glancing aft to see John Ruch and Doug Parfet, from Eric's watch, dragging the forestaysail out of the main hatch and forward along the port deck. Down to leeward, up to my shins in water gushing up from the starboard rail, I passed the sheet through a block on the deck and tied the end to a rail near the mast.

We turned to the reef. I lowered the main halyard six feet, and Doug and John pulled the sail down against the force of the wind and secured a ring sewn in its luff under a stainless-steel hook on the boom. Then Doug helped me crank the halyard up taut on the winch. The three of us took turns at winching in the reefing line that ran from the leech into the boom and forward. It was arm-wearying work. With the reef tied in and her mainsail's area decreased by about 15 percent, *Toscana* seemed to straighten up slightly.

Next, the change of headsails. Doug and John pulled the forestaysail out of its bag and, their wet hands slipping on the snaphooks, slowly hanked the sail onto the forestay and then hoisted the sail. Nick trimmed the sail in, on an after winch, cleated the sheet, and came forward to help us douse the number 3 hoisted on the headstay. Doug, John, Nick, and I sat down shoulder to shoulder on the foredeck, facing to leeward with our safety harnesses hooked onto the jackwires. We grabbed at the foot of the sail, but the wind stretched it like sheet metal and we could not grip the cloth.

"Eric," I yelled aft, "bear off, bear off!"

A wave broke over the bow and our heads and shoved the four of us to leeward into the lifelines, our safety harness tethers stretched to their limits. With water trickling under our clothes and sea boots, we untangled ourselves from the lifelines and climbed back uphill. The boat leveled as Eric steered her off the wind. When we grabbed the jib again, its cloth softened as it was blanketed by the mainsail. Aft, Susan cast off the halyard. The wind and friction in the slot into which the luff was fed at first kept the sail from coming down. John and Doug slid forward and pulled together on the luff, and the sail gradually dropped in six-foot folds into Nick's lap and mine, and we smothered the heavy Dacron cloth with our bodies. Eric headed back up to the course to the Rock.

"Damn," Doug shouted, "the sail's stuck in the groove!" A few inches of the luff had jammed. If we were unable to free it, we would have to lash the sail on deck, where it would catch wind and water and eventually blow overboard, taking the lifelines and possibly even the stanchions with it.

"We'll cut it away," Doug said. I tossed him my knife and he slit the sail just above the jam-up and pulled the luff out of the slot. He opened the halyard shackle, shook the sail's head out, and secured the shackle to the bow pulpit, the stainless-steel thigh-high cage that all this time had restrained him from being washed or heaved overboard as the bow lifted and plunged through a ten-foot arc.

While we held the jib on deck, Doug crawled aft and opened the forward hatch. We slowly stuffed the sail below, first with our arms and then with our legs. Waves broke on deck and water poured into the forward cabin down the creases and folds. When the sail was entirely below, John dropped through the hatch and, from inside, closed and locked the cover.

Susan, in the cockpit, yelled something.

"What?" I shouted back.

"How's the trim on the staysail?" She was still racing.

"I can't see. Where's a light?" Somebody shined a large torch on the sail.

"On course, a little high, a little low, on course," Eric chanted as the waves threw *Toscana* either side of our course.

"Ease it out a little," I yelled aft. When the shape looked right at a moment when Eric said, "On course," I shouted to Susan, "That's fine. Hold that."

We unhooked ourselves and walked aft, sliding our hands along the lifelines and crouching like boxers to absorb the motion of the deck, which tried to propel us into the nearest wave.

We were soaked after our half hour's work on the foredeck. Stumbling into the cockpit as a wave smashed the boat amidships, I slid under the safety line to the low side and around the steering wheel.

*"Keep your harnesses hooked on, damnit!"* Eric said in as near a roar as his gentle voice could command.

When I touched the wheel with my right hand, the palm of the wet leather glove slid across the elk hide cover that insulated the helmsman's fingers from the cold stainless steel of the wheel's outer rim. I squeezed the rim tighter and said, "I've got her, Eric."

He sidestepped uphill to windward and I followed, grabbing the wheel with my left hand where he released it with his right. The wheel turned through twenty degrees as we rocked and pitched. When Eric released his grip entirely, I slid my left hand to where his had been, at the ten o'clock position. With my right hand at three o'clock, I could turn the wheel clockwise to keep the boat from rounding up when waves struck her admidships and she heeled. When the waves slid under her transom and we surfed off course, I pulled the wheel counterclockwise to bring her up. I had never worked harder at steering a boat. The instrument dials now read: wind speed—forty-five, forty-three, forty-six knots; relative wind angle—ninety, one hundred, eighty-five degrees; boat speed—8.61, 9.20, 8.83, 9.45 knots. We had traded some speed for improved control.

Eric's watch went below. After half an hour, we were again overpowered: too great of an angle of heel, and excessive strain on the rudder.

"Get the navigator on deck to take the wheel," I told Susan. "We have to tie the third reef in."

She opened the hatch and stuck her head below. Almost before she had finished passing along the message, John Coote was on deck in his bright blue foul-weather gear.

"The zero-zero-fifteen shipping bulletin predicts force 9 to force 10 from the south-west, veering to north-west," he said as he crawled into the cockpit. "It looks as though we have force 9 already."

"What's the barometer?" I asked.

"Down to 986 at Valentia, rapidly falling." The barometer had dropped nineteen millibars, or half an inch, in only seven hours. The clouds had been right.

"Could you steer while we try to tie in the third reef?" I asked Coote.

"Gladly."

"We'll have to lower the main," I told him.

"Good luck," Coote said as he took the wheel.

Nick and John went forward to the base of the mast to lower the mainsail. We had only two reefing lines at the outer end of the boom. One, which was red, was holding down the second reef that we had just tied. The other, which was green, held down the first reef and was now redundant, since the second reef had superseded it (reefs in mainsails are like slats in venetian blinds; as each reef is tied in, several more feet of sail are removed from the flow of the wind). We had to pull the green reefing line out of the first reef and lead it through the third reef, but to get at the line, we would have to be able to get at the end of the boom, which was now ten feet to leeward, tripping through waves.

As Nick and John pulled the mainsail down, Susan and I trimmed the mainsheet until the boom was waving over our heads. Most of the sail flogged to leeward. I stood on the cabin top, hooked my harness into the safety line, and leaned over the boom to steady it. I pulled at the green line, but, wedged under the red line in the second reef, it would not budge.

"Ease the red line," I yelled forward. Only twenty feet away, they did not hear a word I said. "*Ease the red line!*" I screamed. Nick looked at me, trying to read my lips. "Goddammit, the *RED* line, *ease the RED LINE!*"

Nick knelt down on deck and reached for a winch. The green line went slack.

"No, the red one, the *OTHER* one!"

He nodded and reached for another winch. The red line eased out.

"That's enough!" I showed Nick the palm of my left hand and

he cleated the line. I freed the green line and reached far over the boom for the third reef cringle, a heavy steel ring. The cringle flapped wildly and banged my fingers. I thought, even in twenty knots of wind this would be not easy. I finally grabbed the cringle with the middle finger of my left hand, held it long enough to pass the green line through it, and then pulled the line back to the boom and, using a bowline knot, secured the end through a metal plate.

"It's made!" I shouted, and I crawled off the boom and into the cockpit. Coote, behind me, whistled a loud sigh of relief. Nick and John tied down the cringle in the luff and winched the mainsail up. The head seemed barely halfway up the mast. Susan eased the mainsheet, and the men forward pulled down the leech cringle with the green line, led around a winch.

I relieved Coote at the helm. "You know," he said, "we were going along quite nicely with only the forestaysail up." Nick and John came aft and, panting, threw themselves down on the windward cockpit seat.

Continuing to increase, the wind was now in the mid to high fifties. We were going no slower yet the steering was slightly easier even though the waves came in confusing patterns and at times tossed the boat around wildly. After a while I said, "I hope you don't mind, but I think I should do most of the steering. Let's keep two people on deck. The other two can go below to warm up." I was chilled.

"Go ahead," Nick said. "If you get tired, let me know." Nobody went below.

As the wind built over the next two hours, the seas continued to grow larger. They broke with surprising frequency. For a while, I watched for the big ones over my left, windward, shoulder and tried to steer down their faces so they would not break over us. *Toscana* was not too large to be rolled over by a wave. A sixty-one-footer, *Sorcery*, was rolled in the North Pacific in 1976 and her mast, rigging, and lifelines were swept overboard as though a huge knife had sliced along her deck. In a confused sea like this one, churned up by a rapidly building and shifting wind blowing over relatively shallow water, there was always the chance of a giant wave rearing over and capsizing us.

But the night was too dark, the bad waves were too frequent, and I was too awed to continue the lookout. Their great size and speed distracted me from steering. Yet with my eyes straining ahead, I could still sense from the motion of the boat and increasing volume of the roar when the bad ones were coming, like moving walls, and would shout warnings to my watchmates who sat huddled in the cockpit. They could only pull their heads into their foul-weather jackets and parkas and hold on tight. One wave broke over us, knocking my glasses off until they dangled by the safety strap, collapsing my wool hat over my face, and filling the cockpit. Another big one slid out from under us and *Toscana* fell into the next trough with a crash that dislodged the lock on the forward hatch and opened the cover halfway, letting in a flood of water. John went below to close the cover and to pump.

For the first two hours, the only steady lights were those in the instrument dials, which I could barely make out through my soaked glasses, and the port running light on the bow, which turned the forward waves red. After a bad breaker smashed into the man-overboard light that hung on the lifelines behind my back, the light turned on as it flipped into the cockpit. Its flashing strobe had us helplessly blinded until John muffled it and turned it off.

For a frightening moment, we saw a green running light ahead, which indicated that we were on a collision course with a boat heading back from the Rock. The light disappeared for a couple of minutes and then showed up again down to leeward. A collision between two boats each going over nine knots would have been fatal to both. The sky briefly cleared at about 1:30, revealing a half-moon with its crescent, oddly, facing down. I thought, that's the center of the depression.

Coote had told us to begin looking for Fastnet Rock light at 2:00 A.M., when we should have been within its eighteen-mile range, but it did not appear until almost an hour later. Instead of dead ahead, it was fifteen degrees on the port bow—we had been pushed to leeward farther than anticipated. As we trimmed the sails and headed up, the wind continued on the gradual veer that had started just after midnight. Instead of reaching at nine and a half knots in a south-westerly, we were now beating at six knots into a north-westerly, still not making the course to the Rock. *Toscana*'s bow started to pound into waves from the new direction. I thought, I've never seen worse, but God save the little boats. *Toscana* was stable enough to carry sail to keep her speed up in this sea and wind, but a thirty-five-footer could carry little or no sail area upwind in force 9 or more. With little speed, she could not be steered around the worst waves and could be badly battered.

Eric and his watch relieved us at 3:00 A.M. Cold and stiff, we went below. As I slowly peeled off the layers of sodden clothes, I heard the normally imperturbable Coote shout, "That's Clear Island and it's only a mile and a half to leeward. Tack! Tack *now!*" The bow swung through the eye of the wind with a roar of waves and wildly flogging sails. The staysail continued to flap after we were around. "The sheet's untied," I heard Sherry shout. Running feet pounded forward. I crawled into the sleeping bag. My shoulders ached and I shivered with cold. I pulled my knees up under my chin in the fetal position and instantly went to sleep.

Sometime later, I was awakened by a light shining through a porthole. Coote was shouting, "We're clear now, Eric. You can bear off to course."

I sat up and looked out the port. To leeward was Fastnet Rock, its baroque lighthouse almost hidden by spray. Between *Toscana* and it sailed a small cruising boat plugging along through the waves with only a storm jib up. I heard Eric, in the cockpit, say with amazement, "What could that little boat be doing out here on such a night?"

# 5 TROPHY: Slipping Away

**T**HE FIRST to round Fastnet Rock was the largest yacht in the fleet, *Kialoa*, at 12:45 Monday afternoon. Sixteen hours later, as we in *Toscana* prepared to make the turn and head back to England, this American seventy-nine-foot sloop was approaching the Isles of Scilly. Her passage across the Western Approaches had been quick but eventful.

When the wind built late Monday night, whipping through forces 7, 8, 9, and 10 in two hours, *Kialoa's* crew shortened sail as quickly as the enormous forces on her equipment would allow. By midnight, she was sailing under triple-reefed mainsail and number-3 jib, and two-thirds of her twenty-man crew were on deck in anticipation of further changes. Soon after, they lowered the number-3 jib and raised the number 4; later they changed to the forestaysail.

*Kialoa* reveled in these conditions. Her owner, a Los Angeles real estate executive named John Kilroy, had had her built for offshore racing. Since her launching in 1974, she had made two circumnavigations of the world in search of hard racing, winning the World Ocean Racing Championship along with dozens of races. A man who thoroughly enjoyed the power that his wealth had provided him, Kilroy—like many owners of large yachts—had made his vessel into an extension of his own personality. He had closely supervised the designers and builders he had commissioned to create her and had gone to great lengths to evaluate her performance with computers and other sophisticated electronic instruments.

Kilroy was proud of his knowledge of both his yacht and her equipment. Therefore, he was surprised when a block on the windward running backstay broke—a fitting that had been designed to take a load of twenty-four thousand pounds. With the backstay slack, her ninety-five-foot mast was inadequately supported between its top and the deck. As *Kialoa* pounded over the waves at speeds of well over ten knots, the middle of her mast swayed fore and aft through an arc of four feet. Knowing it was only a matter of moments before the spar would snap, Kilroy ordered the mainsail trimmed all the way. The pressure of the sail would provide some support until an emergency backstay could be rigged. The mast steadied and held.

Kilroy himself was not so fortunate. A gust that he estimated at seventy knots in strength knocked the big sloop over on her side and, he said later, "a wave that was solid green water at least six feet above the deck picked five guys up and threw them at me." Kilroy was pinned against a winch. In considerable pain, he extracted himself from the heap of men and went below, where he stayed for much of the remainder of the race. First thought to be broken ribs, the injury was eventually diagnosed as a ruptured chest cartilage by a sports-medicine doctor, who told Kilroy that he now had something in common with American football quarterbacks who are tackled by burly defensemen.

Kilroy suffered one more embarrassment. *Kialoa* was caught and beaten to the finish at Plymouth by the seventy-seven-footer *Condor of Bermuda*, whose crew not only sailed closer to the Isles of Scilly than the more conservative Kilroy but also set a spinnaker when the wind dropped down to forty knots. Despite a broken spinnaker sheet block and several wild broaches when she was overpowered by gusts (at one stage, she spun through 180 degrees and started sailing backward at three knots), *Condor* kept on under the big sail at speeds as high as twenty-nine knots until she submarined her entire forward deck under a wave. The spinnaker was then lowered.

*Condor* beat *Kialoa* to Plymouth by twenty-eight minutes and broke the Fastnet race elapsed-time record by almost eight hours. Rob James, one of her crew members and a crew and skipper in two round-the-world races, said after the finish that the waves had been worse than any he had experienced around Cape Horn or in the southern oceans—two areas famous for dangerous seas.

In the 170 miles of water between *Toscana* and the two lead-

ing boats—all three of whose crews were able to keep racing—
there were dozens of crews whose concerns were considerably
more basic than that of sailing fast. Some were able to stay on
course under storm sails. One of these was the crew of *Imp,* an
American thirty-nine-footer, who were content to sail under
deeply reefed mainsail alone for several hours, averaging a
speed of about seven knots—fast enough to allow good steering,
yet slow enough to stay in control. Her owner, Dave Allen,
figured correctly that simply being able to finish the race would
assure *Imp* a good position in the Fastnet and Admiral's Cup
placings (of the 303 starters, only 85 finished; 41 of the 54
Admiral's Cup yachts that started finished the race). Fast
enough in the early part of the race to have reached Fastnet
Rock before the wind veered to the north-west, *Imp,* unlike
*Toscana* and the vast majority of other boats, never had to try to
beat into the gale. Likewise with *Eclipse,* an English thirty-
nine-footer, which, under storm jib and double-reefed mainsail,
was rolled over on her side by a wave when twelve miles from
the Rock, at about 1:00 A.M. Tuesday. The crew lowered the
mainsail for a while, and after some discussion, the third reef
was tied in and the sail was rehoisted. Once around the Rock,
the crew even considered hoisting the larger, number-4 jib, but
the wind strengthened to the point where they lowered the
mainsail once again and sailed under jib alone relatively comfortably at seven knots. *Imp,* which went for stretches under
mainsail alone, finished seventh on handicap in the race; *Eclipse,*
under a different sail for the same reason, finished second. Their
elapsed times differed by only seven minutes.

Another, much larger, category included all the boats that
were not fast enough to have reached the Rock before the wind
shifted to the west. Many, unlike *Toscana,* were not sufficiently
large and stable to carry sail while beating to windward in such a
strong wind. Most of these boats were smaller than about forty
feet (*Imp* and *Eclipse* were exceptionally fast for their thirty-
nine-foot length), as were the majority of the boats in the fleet.

*Windswept* went through an ordeal that was in many ways
typical of the experiences of many of these boats. Her crew was

of average ability—some members widely experienced, others not much more than novices. She was handled conservatively. And she suffered two major and several minor misfortunes.

Owned by George Tinley, a very knowledgeable sailor from Lymington, *Windswept* was one of the boats in the new Offshore One-Design-34 Class designed by an American, Doug Peterson, and built by an Englishman, Jeremy Rogers, who also built and owned the successful *Eclipse*. Tinley's crew consisted of six sailors, some old friends, others recent acquaintances. Many ocean-racing skippers prefer to take friends as crew members, not only to enjoy their companionship but also because the mutual understanding and respect of their relationship may allow for better teamwork. Others make a point of not inviting friends to crew so that personal loyalties will not intrude. Crewing for Tinley in *Windswept* were a small-boat-racing sailor with limited offshore experience; a man with whom the skipper had raced in small boats twenty-five years earlier ("A marvelous chap to be out with," Tinley said of him); a young apprentice sailmaker who had sailed in *Windswept* in three offshore races in 1979; a young Frenchwoman with some offshore sailing experience; a knowledgeable navigator; and a sixteen-year-old boy who had sailed a great deal with his parents.

When conditions deteriorated on Monday evening, the crew quickly shortened sail until at 1:00 A.M. *Windswept* was sailing under storm jib alone, going fast and in control, although the mast shook violently when she was battered by the seas. As the wind continued to build, reaching sixty knots on *Windswept's* anemometer, Tinley decided to lower the storm jib and let the boat lie a-hull, letting her lie with no speed on with her port side to the waves so she could bob up and down. This is an established technique for riding out storms. Two crew members kept a lookout in the cockpit, their safety harnesses securely snapped to a safety line, but they did not wear life jackets. Nobody was badly seasick, the motion was comfortable, and the deck was dry. At one stage the Frenchwoman told Tinley that the experience reminded her of sitting on a beach and watching the waves harmlessly come in. "We were just lying there like a little duck, going up and down," Tinley said later, "which is just what all the books say should happen."

The only problem was the cold. Sitting inactive in the cockpit, with the tiller lashed to leeward, the lookouts began to suffer. Sometime between 3:00 and 4:00 A.M., Tinley called for a change of watch, and he and the woman were replaced by two men who had been warming up below.

Soon after the watch change, with no warning, a huge wave rolled *Windswept* over and threw the lookouts out of the boat to the limit of their safety harness tethers. One, Alan Ford, was able to crawl back relatively easily as the boat righted herself. The other, Charles Warren, had considerable difficulty climbing up the high topsides and over the lifelines. Below, everybody was thrown onto a leeward berth. Tinley's nose was broken, and through the dim glow of the single lamp that was lit—its globe was full of water, creating a weird effect—the others could see his blood mingling with gallons of water that had made its way into the cabin. Glass jars had broken and the interior was a mess.

Having seen that lying a-hull was not effective, Tinley decided to run out a drogue, or sea anchor, to try to keep *Windswept's* bow pointed into the waves so she would not be rolled over sideways again—another traditional storm tactic. They tied lines and an anchor around a sail in its bag and threw the improvised drogue off the bow on the end of a large mooring line. The boat drifted faster than the drogue and eventually came up short against the line, which pulled the bow almost directly into the waves. The motion was considerably more comfortable, so all seven crew members retired to the relative warmth of the cabin. Every five minutes, somebody would look out the companionway hatch. A lookout soon spotted another boat gradually approaching through the waves. The navigator lit a white flare, and Tinley started the engine, put it in gear, and steered to port. The other boat drifted by, and *Windswept*, with the starboard side of her bow now to windward, felt even more comfortable.

Tinley lashed the tiller to port, the new leeward side, moved the uninflated life raft from its locker to the cockpit sole, where he lashed it down, and issued inflatable life jackets, one of which, though brand new, was already punctured.

Soon after, confused waves smashed the bow back across and, with the tiller now to windward, the boat's bow continued to swing off until *Windswept* once again had the seas on her beam. Tinley started the engine and threw it into gear, only to feel the propeller grind to a halt as it was entangled by a line streaming overboard. There was not much that Tinley could do except relash the helm to leeward and return below.

Not long after, a wave lifted *Windswept*'s bow and smashed her completely upside down.

In the capsize, Tinley, already bloodied, suffered a broken wrist and was knocked unconscious. He had been sitting on sail bags on the cabin sole, eating a piece of chocolate. He has no recollection of where he ended up, but he knows that one of his shipmates was thrown from a bunk into the forward cabin, leaving footprints on the main cabin's ceiling. *Windswept* remained upside down long enough for the rest of the crew to start worrying. "Never mind," somebody shouted, "it will come up again in a minute!" For thirty seconds or more, the horrified crew sat or lay in pitch darkness, hearing water rush through the companionway hatch (one washboard had been left open to provide air below), through air vents in the deck, and through the cockpit seats. When she finally righted herself, the water was up to the level of the settee berths, at least two feet above the bilge.

The bilge pump handle had disappeared during the capsize, so two people began bailing out the cabin with buckets. On deck, other crew members found the life raft, still uninflated and dragging overboard at the end of the inflation line. Apparently planning to abandon the yacht, they hauled the raft back on board and tugged on the line until it broke at the $CO_2$ bottle. Obviously, their only life raft would have to be *Windswept* herself, and she did not seem very fit for sea. As men below bailed water into the cockpit, loose tea bags and other debris clogged the cockpit drains until the cockpit itself filled and the water started to spill back into the cabin through the seat lockers. The engine was useless, the batteries were leaking a smelly acid, all the lights were out, and the skipper was lying unconscious in the cabin. Lying next to him, Charles Warren, who had suffered a broken nose and been stunned, assumed that the boat had split open and was sinking—he knew nothing of the capsize. When Tinley regained consciousness, he was in the cockpit, his safety harness hooked onto a line. Nobody knew how he had arrived there.

The boat rode relatively easy, yet the seven sailors were unanimous in thinking that they had to get off *Windswept*. "Lives being more important than boats," Tinley later said, "we would be taken off." But there was no getting off without the life raft and, without a radio transmitter, no way to call for help. The sailors attempted to inflate the raft with a small hand pump before giving up after six hours. They moved the drogue line aft to the transom to keep the stern square to the waves, and shot off red flares as the sky began to brighten. Soom, a mast appeared, and a sister ship named *Mickey Mouse* careened down the seas toward them. In those conditions, *Mickey Mouse* could offer little aid, although her crew did shoot off a flare to try to attract the attention of a trawler that passed a few hundred yards away. *Windswept's* crew fired four red parachute flares, one of which did not function.

Alan Ford, the small-boat sailor who had the least amount of experience in offshore sailing, took the tiller and steered skillfully for the next four hours. Her speed limited by the drogue, *Windswept* was manageable and did not threaten to pitchpole, or somersault over her bow, while racing down the steep waves. The 360 feet of line, the sail bag, and the anchor were finally working. Tinley tied a six-gallon jerry can of fresh water to the line to increase the resistance. "We found that if she was carried off really fast on the face of a wave and the helmsman made a mistake, we were really done," he said later. Although morale was low, the crew continued to try to improve the drogue, even hanging out loops of line to break waves before they reached the boat, an idea that they had read about in boating magazines and that they found was unsuccessful in practice.

The interior, though dry, was useless for sleeping. The lee cloths that had cocooned sleepers in the main cabin settees had broken, and the only useful bunks were the underdeck pilot berths, which nobody wanted to use for fear of being trapped if the boat capsized again. The crew huddled together on the cabin sole for warmth, and from time to time the Frenchwoman ("The good Sophie," Tinley called her) blew warm air down their shirt fronts. All day Tuesday, *Windswept*'s cold, disheartened crew took turns steering and trying to rest in the cabin. They realized in late afternoon that the wind was dying and prepared to get under sail. Since they were uncertain of their position, Tinley worried about making a landfall on the unfamiliar coast of southern Ireland. At about 5:00 P.M., they attracted another racing boat by waving an SOS flag that they had prepared from a lee cloth to signal helicopters. The boat passed close by and her crew gave Tinley the compass course to Kinsale. It was dead into the wind, and Tinley decided that *Windswept* could reach with more comfort and speed to Cork. After using sheet winches to haul in the drogue, they set the storm jib and were under way. It was a slow, long sail until they had recovered enough from the shock of the storm to set the much larger number-2 jib at dawn on Wednesday for the last, increasingly pleasant, twenty-five miles into Crosshaven, the yachting harbor of Cork, Ireland.

"When men take up a dangerous sport some must expect to die," a reader wrote to the English magazine *Yachting World* after the Fastnet race. Yet unlike mountaineers and race-car drivers, few of the people in *Windswept*'s crew or in the Fastnet fleet would have called their sport dangerous before the gale broke over them Monday night—frequently uncomfortable and sometimes harrowing, but rarely if ever a threat to life and limb.

Ocean racing's record of fatalities was probably shorter than forty people in over one hundred years. From time to time, individuals had been lost off boats or had been fatally injured during races. The death of Colonel Hudson in the 1931 Fastnet race was such a fatality, and during the Southern Ocean Racing Conference series held off Florida in 1979, one man fell off the stern of a boat at night and drowned and another man died after a

boom fractured his skull. During the first ocean race ever held, a
transatlantic race between three one-hundred-foot schooners, in
December 1866, a wave swept six men out of *Fleetwing*'s cockpit. This was the greatest loss of life from a racing crew until a
French thirty-five-footer, *Airel*, went down without either a
trace or an explanation during a short race off Marseilles in 1977,
taking seven men with her. Forty-two years earlier, during a
transatlantic race to Norway, an American named Robert Ames
was washed off his ketch *Hamrah* at night during a gale. His son
Richard dove overboard and swam to him, and another son,
Henry, launched a rowboat to rescue them both. The rowboat
capsized and the three men disappeared before *Hamrah*'s remaining three crew members could sail back to them. Frightful
as they were, the *Fleetwing*, *Airel*, and *Hamrah* tragedies, total-
ing sixteen deaths, were so exceptional that most yachtsmen first
hear about them as legendary examples not of the sea's cruelty
but of poor seamanship: *nobody* should race across the North
Atlantic Ocean in December, or sail in a boat, that, like *Airel*, is
not equipped with a life raft, or swim for a man who has fallen
overboard.

Few people who go to sea for pleasure would disagree with a
dogma propounded by Thomas Fleming Day, the founder of
American ocean racing. "The danger of the sea for generations
has been preached by the ignorant," Day wrote some seventy
years before the 1979 Fastnet race; "it has been the theme for
the landsman poet and writer, until the mass of the people have
accepted this gross libel of our Great Green Mother as gospel.
. . . [A seaman] knows well enough that the sea never destroys
purposely and malignantly. He knows that it never has or will
murder a vessel; that every vessel that goes down commits suicide."

Whether or not they got into major trouble, George Tinley
and many other survivors of the Fastnet gale have good reason
to be less trusting of the sea than was Day. Even small mishaps
were threatening to life. On board *Carina*, the successor to the
winner of the 1955 and 1957 races, a lurch sent a carving knife
flying out of a galley drawer, across the main cabin, and, point

first, into a door. When *Aries*'s life raft was thrown from its cockpit storage space, the inflation line tangled in the steering wheel, which, as it turned, triggered the $CO_2$ canister. The crew watched helplessly as the raft filled the cockpit. When it threatened to jam against the wheel, they hacked the raft to pieces with knives and threw it below to be glued back together. The log of *Mosika Alma* read: "0600, FLIPPED UPSIDE DOWN to 180 degrees. No serious injuries. No structural or rigging damage. Skipper cracked ribs, mate smashed nose, one crew facial cuts." As the Royal Navy yacht *Bonaventure II* went through a series of knockdowns just after dawn on Tuesday, her mast became progressively weaker and finally snapped during the third knockdown, hitting and breaking the left forearm of her skipper, Captain Graham Laslett, Royal Navy, and falling on top of three men who had been hurled overboard. Two of the men were quickly cut free and hauled themselves back aboard, but the third was so entangled in the mess of wire, rope, aluminum mast, and sails that his recovery from the water took well over an hour. Spotting a ship that appeared to be on a collision course with *Bonaventure*, Laslett fired off flares and ordered the life raft prepared for quick inflation. The ship altered course at the last moment and stopped; it turned out to be a Royal Navy fishery protection vessel, HMS *Anglesey*, which had been homed in on *Bonaventure* by a Nimrod patrol plane. Laslett decided to abandon ship. His crew inflated the life raft, climbed into it, and drifted downwind to where the *Anglesey* stood by.

These threatening accidents were almost trivial in comparison with the fifteen deaths that occurred on August 14. One fatality was Peter Dorey, who was steering his thirty-seven-footer, *Cavale*, when she was capsized at about 3:00 A.M. while running before the gale under bare poles. He and the other man on deck, Philip Bodman, were heaved overboard. Bodman's safety harness took the strain, but Dorey's did not and he was washed away. Dorey was fifty-one years old, a shipping executive, and the president of the States Advisory and Finance Committee of Guernsey, in the Channel Islands. Before the start of the Fastnet, he had twice put his boat and crew through man-overboard drills, but on that dark night he was out of sight of *Cavale* within moments. On board *Cavale* were one of his sons and a cousin.

Broken equipment also was responsible for the loss of two men from the Royal Naval Engineering College's thirty-five-footer, *Flashlight*. The men, Russell Brown and Charles Stevenson, both Royal Navy officers, were lost when safety harnesses and a lifeline broke. When the Dutch-owned thirty-three-foot Fastnet entry *Veronier II* rolled while hove-to under storm jib, G. J. Williabey and another man were thrown from the cockpit. The rope tether of Williabey's safety harness broke, and the other man, whose harness remained intact, suffered bruises to his body under the harness and to his hands and arms where he grabbed at objects. When the boat righted herself, the crew threw a man-overboard buoy with a strobe light into the water and returned to it. After searching for Williabey for twenty minutes, they decided that he was lost and that they were risking their own lives.

*Festina Tertia*, a British thirty-five-footer on charter, had abandoned the race early on Tuesday morning and was running back toward England under storm jib in excellent control. Her only problem was that the small cockpit drains could not dispose of water quickly enough as waves broke over her. With the cockpit full of water, the seat lockers were filling and draining into the bilge. At about 1:30 P.M., she was unexpectedly rolled 150 degrees by a cresting wave whose only advance warning was the roar of the breaker. One man was thrown so hard against the steering wheel that its supporting column broke. When *Festina Tertia* righted herself, another man, Roger Watts, was missing; his safety harness tether was still hooked to the boat and the harness, which apparently had snapped, was attached to the tether.

The crew immediately started man-overboard procedures, rounding up to Watts, who lay face down and unresponsive in the water. On the third pass, Sean Thrower stripped off his foul-weather gear and outer clothing, dove in, and swam toward the man, but a wave separated them. "Can't you see he's dead!" somebody shouted, and Thrower swam back to the boat. The waves had been forceful enough to rip his underwear off. Suffering from hypothermia, he was hauled into the boat, dried off, and bundled into warm clothes and a sleeping bag. His shipmates realized that he was on the verge of shock, so they radioed a Mayday, and an hour and a half later, a helicopter arrived overhead. The crew inflated the life raft, and Thrower climbed into it and pushed away. The cable pulled him up into the helicopter, and fifteen minutes later he was in a warm bath in the Culdrose sick bay.

The death of a crew member in the thirty-two-foot *Gunslinger* came well after the boat was rolled over. Running before the gale under storm jib early on Tuesday morning, she handled the seas well until her rudder broke. Bob Lloyd, the skipper, opened the hatch and yelled below for help, and was lowering the jib when the boat broached, skidding off sideways down the face of a wave. The succeeding wave rolled her over on her side. Lloyd was thrown overboard, to the end of his tether, and the other crew members come on the deck of the now-righted boat. The next wave rolled the boat over on her side once again, and was followed by a wave as high as forty feet, which curled high above *Gunslinger*, broke, and drove her all the way over. She was upside down.

Water poured through the open hatch, and when the boat finally righted herself, the cabin was flooded to the level of the lower bunks—about knee height—and seemed to be taking on more water. The crew assumed that she was leaking badly through a hole left by the broken rudder. When the water reached waist height, they decided to abandon ship. *Gunslinger* was now more than half filled. One crew member radioed a Mayday; the others inflated the life raft. The raft was pushed overboard, and Paul Baldwin got into it with a flashlight and other equipment as the others prepared to follow.

A breaking wave then swept over the boat and capsized the raft, throwing Baldwin out. The other men watched as he struggled to swim back to the raft, in his life jacket. The bow line of the raft tightened and broke, injuring the hand of the crew member holding it. When his shipmates last saw Paul Baldwin, the raft was drifting away from him.

*Gunslinger* now had to be made seaworthy. The crew bailed

How a boat can be capsized. First, she broaches to one side while surfing down the face of the large wave. The next wave then breaks over her with thousands of pounds of water flying at speeds over thirty knots. As the breaker collapses over her, the boat is lifted over on the face of the wave, until she is rolled upside down with her mast in the water, throwing men out of the cockpit and, sometimes, breaking the mast. Here, *Gunslinger,* the stump of her broken rudder showing, remains capsized until a wave pushes against the keel, which rights her.

frantically, and after a couple of hours the water level in the cabin had dropped. She was not leaking, the crew decided; the added water had poured into the bilge from the lockers, shelves, and head liner. Able to get out a distress call, they attracted a helicopter, which picked an injured crew member, Mike Flowers, out of the water at about 5:00 P.M. The others endured the cold and rolling until 8:30 Wednesday morning, when a Dutch trawler, the *Alidia,* took *Gunslinger* under tow to Crosshaven, where she suffered some damage when she drifted onto a trawler. Aside from the broken rudder, that was the only serious damage that *Gunslinger* suffered during her long ordeal.

Of all the stories of boats and crews distressed during the Fastnet gale, few are more terrifying than that of *Trophy.*

An Oyster thirty-seven-footer designed by the British firm of Holman and Pye, *Trophy* was owned by Alan Bartlett, a North London pub owner who had sailed for over twenty years and who, in *Trophy* and previous boats, had raced in an earlier Fastnet and in several other RORC events. A genial man who cared strongly about his boat and crew, Bartlett had a steady crew of seven men, all of whom had sailed together before the 1979 Fastnet race. During 1978, *Trophy*'s first year, the crew had been worried by apparent structural weaknesses in the boat, and Bartlett had arranged for a boatyard to reinforce the hull—a complicated and expensive procedure that involved the removal of the entire cabin. When *Trophy* was reassembled in the spring of 1979, the crew installed a few special items, among them a custom-built navigator's seat in which they stored flares and other safety equipment. Every weekend, the eight men worked on the boat at Burnham-on-Crouch, about forty miles east of London.

Once the racing season opened, the crew experienced the mix of mediocre and prize-winning performances that is the lot of most ocean-racing boats, winning their class in the ninety-mile race from Harwich to Ostend, Belgium, but doing poorly in the rough conditions of Cowes Week. Like most crews, they spent the day before the Fastnet race start storing food and clothing and checking safety equipment and racing gear. The

Beaufort life raft had been inspected a month or so earlier, and now a crew member carefully examined its storage locker under a seat in the cockpit. To his surprise, he discovered that somebody had screwed down the top of the locker. In the highly unlikely event that they would abandon ship, the crew would have to locate and then use a screwdriver simply to get at the life raft. The man replaced the screws with cotter pins, or split pins, which could easily be pulled out of holes in the locker.

The first two days of the race were slow, the only excitement coming when a tug towing part of an oil rig loomed out of the fog on Sunday and passed close by. When the wind built after Monday morning's flat calm, they were off Land's End, and soon they were flying toward Fastnet Rock under spinnaker. The 12:15 weather forecast of force 6 to 8 did not disturb either Bartlett or his crew, most of whom had been through bad weather in *Trophy* or her predecessors. In fact, it was the rough return from the last race of the 1978 season that had convinced Bartlett that the hull required reinforcement, because as they had sailed across the English Channel under small jib alone, they had felt the hull twisting under them.

By Monday evening, the conditions were difficult enough to warrant something unusual on one of Alan Bartlett's boats, a cold dinner, since the cook could not keep his footing in front of the stove. They shortened sail to keep up with the increasing wind, and by 10:30 *Trophy* was reaching at ten knots under number-3 jib alone. Seasickness was insidiously taking its toll of the crew, and sleep was difficult. As in many racing yachts, there were not enough bunks for the entire off-watch, so one or two men slept on the sails packed on the sole of the main cabin. Those on deck were hooked onto the lifelines and stanchions with their safety harness, and life jackets were issued.

At about 11:00 the crew on deck spotted a red flare drifting down out of the clouds. Immediately deciding to go to the assistance of the distressed vessel, Bartlett took a compass bearing on the spot from which the flare appeared to have been fired and turned on the engine. He shouted below for somebody to enter the time and position in the logbook. After the finish, he said, he would present the logbook as evidence when asking the race officials for redress for time spent in his rescue efforts. *Trophy's* forty-horsepower diesel drove her well across the waves, beam-to, yet it was still over an hour before she was alongside a dismasted white sloop, whose crew told Bartlett through a series of gestures that all was well, after all. With Simon Fleming at the steering wheel, *Trophy* stayed on station making a bare one knot under power alone.

Also standing by was *Morningtown*, a thirty-nine-foot cruising ketch owned by Rodney Hill and serving as the Royal Ocean Racing Club's official race escort vessel. Her assigned job was to monitor radio channels and to take position reports from the Admiral's Cup yachts. In her crew was Pat Wells, who might have been competing in the race except that his own boat had run aground on the Dutch shore during the North Sea Race in May and had been filled and destroyed by breakers.

*Morningtown* rolled badly in the confused, wild sea, and her crew found it hard to hold her on station, since she made considerable leeway, slipping sideways downwind at over three knots. Peering through the spray-filled gloom, they saw *Trophy* standing by the dismasted sloop, whose crew appeared to be preparing to abandon her in a life raft that they had hauled onto the foredeck. Another flare appeared from a different direction, so *Morningtown's* crew, believing that the disabled boat was being properly shepherded, headed away.

Not long after, *Morningtown's* steering cable slipped off the rudder quadrant and she lay uncomfortably rolling, her beam to the seas, while her crew tried to repair the damage. Looking up, somebody saw a dismasted yacht pass by, and a life raft in the water. To their considerable surprise, the RORC representatives realized that the disabled vessel was *Trophy*, and that she had been abandoned by her crew, who only minutes before had seemed to be in full control.

They *had* been in full control until they slowed down near the first disabled yacht. Only moments after the other crew signaled assurances, *Trophy*, lying almost motionless, was deluged by a huge breaking wave, the force of which spun the steering wheel out of Simon Fleming's hands and whipped the boat around like a wind vane in a gust. When Fleming was able to get his hands back on the wheel, he could not budge it. The rudder, he guessed, had bent and was now jammed at a thirty-degree angle against the boat's bottom. Having decided that there was little they could do, *Trophy*'s crew set to riding out the storm. Three men stood watch in the cockpit and the others went below to try to get some rest. Two of the three washboards were inserted in the companionway behind them to seal the cabin off from the spray and occasional solid water that came on deck. The small opening left by the absent board allowed fresh air in. Simon Fleming lay down on the sail bags and the others crawled into bunks. From his position deep in the hull, Fleming felt the boat to be safe. But very soon after, a wave that the men on deck said roared up as high as the fifty-foot mast broke on *Trophy*, rolling her right over.

Fleming found himself lying on the yacht's overhead, under hundreds of pounds of sails. Robin Bowyer was shouting for help, the fluorescent lights dimmed, and the engine stopped. Fleming fought himself out from under the sails just as the boat righted herself and he was buried once again on the cabin sole under the sails, at least two feet of water, and a heap of equipment that had spilled out of lockers and the navigator's seat. The water had poured through the small hole in the companionway where the extra washboard should have been, and when one of the men on deck pulled out another washboard to look below, more water came down.

On deck, the primary worry had been to avoid colliding with the drifting *Morningtown*, whose crew was out of sight, but when the great wave hit and rolled *Trophy* over, breaking her rigging and wrapping the mast under and around her bow, the escort boat was forgotten. As *Trophy* went over, Russell Smith was trapped in the water under the cockpit, and Richard Mann and Alan Bartlett were thrown clear. Smith and Mann pulled themselves aboard as the boat righted herself, but Bartlett was left dragging overboard by his tether.

Once he had dug himself out from under the sails, Fleming

crawled up the companionway and into the cockpit. Without the weight of the mast aloft, the boat rolled much more quickly now, and the boom, sails, lines, and heaps of other gear that littered her deck swung back and forth across the cockpit, creating hazards for the dazed, confused men trying to keep their footing. Fleming saw Bartlett in the water on the windward side, his life jacket and safety harness entwined in sheets and halyards as he fought to keep his head above water. Fleming tried to haul Bartlett aboard, but the stocky skipper was made heavier by his water-soaked clothes and by the entangling lines. Fleming was, however, able to pull Bartlett alongside and, with Derek Morland, succeeded in hauling his skipper's feet up over the toe rail. Lying in the water with his heels over the rail and his body being hammered against the topsides by the waves, Bartlett thought to himself, "What a silly way to die."

Struggling desperately for a way to get Bartlett aboard, Fleming finally decided to cut him free. He found a knife and hacked away at the lines, slashing the safety harness and life jacket as well, until after ten minutes Bartlett was hauled on deck, exhausted.

Meanwhile, with their skipper over the side and for all intents and purposes out of commission, two other members of the crew took it upon themselves to decide to abandon ship—possibly these men were John Puxley and Peter Everson, who had suffered greatly from seasickness. When Fleming and Morland finally had Bartlett on board, they turned around and saw the inflated life raft in the water to leeward with the two men either in it or climbing into it.

Once inflated, the raft would either have to be cut loose or used. Keeping it on deck or alongside in a sixty-knot wind and thirty-foot seas was an impossibility. Given the situation, Bartlett and his crew had little choice: *Trophy* was dismasted and rolling violently; water was up to her bunks; the blackness of the night was broken only by the white crests of the great breaking waves; rescue was at hand with *Morningtown* nearby and—especially—with the recently inspected, inflated life raft alongside. Alan Bartlett decided to put his faith in the raft.

One by one, the men carefully climbed down into the raft, entering the canopy through the small observation port or through the flap that served as a door. One man brought along a galley knife, and when all eight were aboard, he cut the bowline. The men cautiously passed the knife from hand to hand, keeping the sharp blade away from the two inflated rings until it was dropped overboard. The raft and *Trophy* quickly separated.

Almost immediately, the men again saw *Morningtown*. The crippled ketch drifted down on the life raft from windward. Standing on the foredeck of the thirty-nine-footer, Pat Wells was ready to help them come aboard, but the ginger-bearded Simon Fleming stuck his head out of the canopy door and shouted that they wanted to stay in the raft. Wells was not surprised. *Morningtown* was rolling wildly as she drifted out of control, and the raft seemed to be relatively secure. Having been in a life raft earlier in the year after his own boat had foundered, Wells knew that crew transfers could be risky. His and everybody else's main worry was whether *Morningtown* would run the raft over, but the two boats passed almost within two arms' length, and were soon far apart. The time was about 2:30 A.M.

Before *Morningtown* was out of sight, *Trophy*'s crew had reason to suspect that they had made the wrong decision. Although they felt safe and secure—especially when they saw *Morningtown* go through a series of frightening rail-to-rail rolls—they had trouble getting settled in the raft. They could neither find handholds to which they could clip their safety harnesses, nor locate the drogue, which when thrown overboard would slow the raft as it surfed down the waves. As they settled themselves, the raft went up a particularly steep wave, an edge of the bottom was exposed to the wind, and the raft was flipped over onto its top, spilling four men out into the water. Almost immediately, the raft was blown back upright and the men clambered back aboard. The raft capsized several times more within the next few minutes.

On the fifth capsize, incredibly, the life raft split apart, the two inflated rings detaching from each other. *Morningtown*'s running lights were still within sight, but the ketch was far

Simon Fleming yells to Pat Wells, on *Morningtown*'s forward deck, that *Trophy*'s crew
wishes to remain aboard the life raft.

beyond reach in the black gale. Alan Bartlett was thrown the far-
thest, and he swam five yards back to the upper ring. The only
man without a safety harness and life jacket—which had been
destroyed when he was pulled out of the water—Bartlett was tir-
ing.

Moments later, a wave swept away John Puxley and Peter
Everson, and they could not get back. The six men remaining
with the two parts of the raft frantically tried to paddle toward
the two men, but they disappeared into a wave trough and
were not seen alive again. Puxley, a father of two, was a forty-
two-year-old crane operator from Burnham-on-Crouch. Everson, a bachelor in his thirties, worked for an automobile agency
in Billercay, about fifteen miles east of London.

Up to this point, the men had not secured themselves to the
raft, but now those with harnesses clipped the tethers to the
rope handholds on the outside of the top ring. The men sat in
the bottom ring, which had a floor, and towed the top ring
alongside with their tethers. Somebody found the sea anchor,
which was so tightly wound in its line that it had not opened
automatically. When they let it loose, the line twisted around
Russell Smith's hand, tangled in his safety harness, and almost
pulled him away. When it was finally straightened out, the
drogue slowed the raft and steadied its motion, but the line
broke after but a few minutes, and the small flotilla of inflated
rubber rings and people was soon being rolled over, time after
time. After each capsize the six men bobbed back to the water
surface in time to catch the ring with the floor before it blew
away.

Soon after first light, at about 5:30, a Nimrod spotter airplane flew over their heads and dropped a yellow smoke flare.
Just then, they spotted a yacht on the crest of a wave and they
fired off one of the flares they had found in the life raft. To their
dismay, three more flares shot up almost immediately; they
were not the only crew in difficulty, and although they kept
reassuring themselves that *Morningtown* was bound to report
their position, the six men began to be discouraged. Yet by ex-
perimenting, they discovered that if they lunged forward as the

*At left:* **The Dutch destroyer** *Overijssel* **nears the ruined life raft of** *Trophy* **in heavy seas.** *Peter Webster*

*Below:* **Trophy's life raft—what was left of it—alongside the** *Overijssel. Peter Webster*

raft reached the top of a wave, they would force the raft through the breaking crest rather than over it, and the chances of further capsizing were much decreased.

Sometime after sunrise, perhaps as late as 9:00 A.M., a large wave swept over the men and separated the rings. Fleming, who had unhooked his safety harness, came to the surface to find himself alone next to the bottom ring. The other men were yards away, secured to the upper ring. They tried unsuccessfully to paddle toward each other, and one man even attempted to swim the other ring toward Fleming, but they drifted apart.

Alone in the ring, Fleming considered a variety of possibilities. Should he take off his foul-weather jacket and trousers to use as sails? Should he stand up, sit down, or get back in the water? Tired and suffering from leg cramps, he finally decided to sit in the raft and to try to enjoy the warmth of the sun shining through the cold spray on this crisp, almost cloudless, gale-torn morning. Still in his clothes of the night before (he had not even kicked off the sea boots, which restricted his mobility but warmed his feet), Fleming tightened the hood of his foul-weather jacket around his ears, and reflected on his impending death. Though tired and numb with cold, he was angry at himself. He knew death was coming, and he did not worry about it, but he swore at himself for accepting it, for giving in. It seemed so bloody stupid, he thought, to be dying so slowly and with so little pain, slipping slowly away in this cold sea. Although he felt lucky that he hadn't been injured—an injured man might have lived half an hour, and he had survived for six or seven hours— the whole thing seemed absurd to him.

If Simon Fleming could worry about his own attitude toward death, he still had an Englishman's sensitivity to the comfort of his friends. They were floating around in the upper ring, no more secure than they would have been in a large inner tube. At least, he thought, he could rest his feet. He worried for them.

Fleming didn't know it then, but one of those shipmates gave in to the inevitable at about the time these thoughts were running through his head. Robin Bowyer, a forty-four-year-old sailing instructor, weakened swiftly and died. Alan Bartlett told the others that he would be the next to go. Although physically strong, and a sailor and amateur boxer, Bartlett was fifty-three years old, and his experience had been the worst of any that night among *Trophy*'s crew. After his ordeal at the end of his tether before the boat was abandoned, he had been in the water without a life jacket for hours.

And then came rescue. When Simon Fleming first saw a helicopter, he swore: it seemed to be flying away from him. But it swung back overhead and dropped a man with a sling down to him on a cable, and soon he was in the cabin. A few minutes later, the helicopter hovered over the other ring and picked up Alan Bartlett. The others would soon be recovered by the Dutch destroyer *Overijessel*, which was standing by a few hundred yards away, her crew aghast at the sight of the broken life raft. When Bartlett was hauled into the helicopter's cabin, he was unable to move; he had been in the water for eight hours. The same helicopter, Sea King-597, had also picked up three survivors from *Grimalkin* from their life raft. Bartlett recovered quickly, and the five men were able to walk off the helicopter when it reached Culdrose. The pilot told Simon Fleming that, having seen the remains of their life raft, he was surprised that any of *Trophy*'s eight men had survived.

# 6 The Seas: The Most Fearsome Things

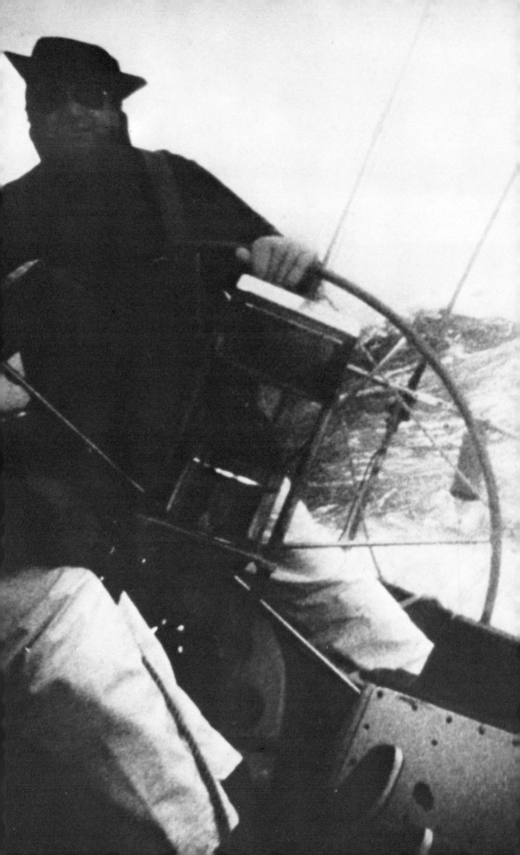

**B**Y DAWN, any anemometers still functioning indicated wind speeds that averaged in the high fifties. Since most of these instruments read no higher than sixty knots, the sailors could only estimate the power of the gusts that pegged the pointers to their limits. Highly experienced men said later that the wind peaked in the seventies—force 12, or hurricane strength. It was a wind that blew down walls and trees all over Britain, killing several people; that swept a radio antenna off *Toscana*'s masthead; that made breathing difficult; that numbed faces. Its full blast, wrote Major J.K.C. Maclean, of the army yacht *Fluter*, created "a shriek of wind that I have only heard before when putting out from the shelter of a boulder on a Scottish hilltop."

But the worst that the wind did was to be the primary cause of a huge, vicious, boat-flipping, morale-shattering seaway. The helicopter pilots, who, while hovering, had to dodge them, said the waves were as high as fifty feet. If that estimate were true, it still misses the point, for the danger of the waves lay not in their height but in their shape. "At daybreak the seas were spectacular," remembered Peter Bruce, a commander in the Royal Navy who was navigator in *Eclipse*. "They had become very large, very steep, and broke awkwardly, but the boat was handling well." George Tinley, who had been so badly beaten around in his *Windswept*, later said, "There were seas coming at one angle with breakers on them, but there were seas coming at another angle also with breakers, and then there were the most fearsome things where the two met in the middle." After the gale, Major Maclean vividly described the appearance of the waves at night: "All around were white horses with their spray flurrying

---

PRECEDING PHOTOGRAPH: *Tenacious* rolls to leeward as she runs under shortened sail on Tuesday morning. *Greg Shires*

horizontally and slashing against us with the added impetus of the occasional rain squalls. But these white horses were just the top of some monster waves which hunched up, their tops flaring with spume, and marched on leaving us high at one minute so we could glimpse around, and then bringing us some fifty feet down into their troughs so we could appreciate the enormity of the next wave following. Some waves had boiling foam all over them where they were moving through the break of a previous wave, or, when the foam had fizzled away, they were deep green from the disturbance of the water. Otherwise the sea was black."

The seas and not the wind gusts were capsizing boats and life rafts and smashing sailors overboard. The wind's strength was such that smaller boats could not carry enough sail to steer around waves or to mitigate their great shocks; yet the seas were the true killers on August 14. Salt water weighs sixty-four pounds per cubic foot, and a moderately large breaker that is six feet high, ten feet across, and six feet thick carries, at a speed as high as thirty knots, twenty-three thousand pounds of water. The average boat in the Fastnet race weighed considerably less than that. When a wave of such size and velocity breaks over a boat like a breaker on an Hawaiian beach, its force overwhelms the stability provided by the hull's shape and the keel. The un-lucky vessel rolls perhaps through ninety degrees, perhaps all the way.

These waves battered even large yachts. The seventy-nine-foot *Kialoa* was knocked over by one, and, according to her de-signer and skipper, German Frers, Jr., *Acadia*, a fifty-one-foot American boat under charter to an Argentinian crew, was twice rolled over so far that her leeward spreaders dipped in the water. The American Admiral's Cupper *Williwaw*, forty-five feet in length, was knocked down while Malin Burnham was climb-ing up the companionway ladder. His feet were swept out from under him with such force that a toenail was sliced off when it hit the underside of the cabin roof. The forty-six-footer *Jan Pott*, a member of the German Admiral's Cup team, was dismasted when she was rolled completely over through 360 degrees. In the thirty-four-foot *Innovation,* a gold crown was shaken off a crew member's tooth, and the owner, Peter Johnson, suffered a broken rib when he was heaved against a bulkhead during one of three bad knockdowns.

The best-known skipper in the Fastnet race, former British prime minister Edward Heath, did not escape problems either. His forty-four-foot *Morning Cloud,* a member of the British Admiral's Cup team, rounded the Rock at 1:30 A.M. About two and a half hours later, a wave so black that nobody saw it coming out of the night smashed down from overhead and rolled her 130 degrees. The helmsman, Larry Marks, was banged first against the steering wheel and then against a stanchion, bending both. Two men were heaved so far that they ended up under the hull, on the ends of the tethers of their safety harnesses. After all were pulled back on deck, Heath decided to take in the deeply reefed mainsail and lie a-hull. *Morning Cloud* eventually got sailing again, but, undoubtedly discouraged by this latest bit of misfortune, after the loss of her rudder in the Channel race and vandalism to the hull during Cowes Week, Heath took it easy. "When daylight came," Marks said later, "we thought, 'Blimey, this is pretty bad.' We were still pretty much dazed, and we all thought that the best thing to do was to sail home and sit by a fireside."

This was not the first bad storm to have hit the British coast, whose reputation for rough weather was both deserved and ancient well before gales helped to destroy the Spanish Armada in 1588, but it was unusual in season and duration. In her book *British Weather Disasters,* Ingrid Holford describes thirty-nine natural catastrophes that have devastated Britain since 1638; only seven of them occurred during July or August. The eleventh edition of *The West Coasts of England and Wales Pilot,* a handbook for seamen using the Western Approaches and the Bristol and St. George's channels, reports that there are force 8 and stronger gales 10 to 20 percent of the time in January and only 2 to 5 percent of the time in July. Eighty percent of all gales in the area blow between October and March and only 20 percent blow during the other six months. The average duration of gales, according to the *Pilot*, is four to six hours in winter and less in summer (the Fastnet gale blew for twenty hours). The Royal Navy hydrographers who wrote this edition of the *Pilot* refused to generalize, but their predecessors summarized the weather neatly in the tenth edition: "The region is very stormy."

It always has been so. Richard Earl of Cornwall, a brother of King Henry II, built Hailes Abbey in Gloucestershire as thanks to God after surviving a storm off the Isles of Scilly in 1242. In *The Isles of Scilly*, Crispin Gill writes of how Scilly Islanders lived off ships wrecked on their rocks in winter and summer gales. (According to the etymologist Eric Partridge, "gale" is related to "yell" through the Old Norse word *gala*—"to sing"— and the Danish word *gal*—"furious." Anybody who has stood on a Scilly hilltop during a gale knows that, like a Scottish hilltop, it endures an especially furious shriek of a song.) In his account "The Cruise of the *Tomtit*," the Victorian novelist Wilkie Collins quotes a letter from a friend whom he invited on a September cruise down the north coast of Cornwall to the Scillies but who declined because the cruise was too near the autumnal equinox, a good time for a gale. "You may meet with a gale that will blow you out of the water," the friend warns. "You are running a risk, in my opinion, of the most senseless kind." Another friend writes, "If I were only a single man, there is nothing I should like better than to join you. But I have a wife and family, and I can't reconcile it to my conscience to risk being drowned." And a third friend advises, "Don't come back bottom upwards."

In late July 1936, a force 10 gale hit the small fleet of boats approaching Britain in a transatlantic race from Bermuda to Cuxhaven, Germany. Ben Ames, an American who sailed in the race in a German yacht, *Hamburg*, described the gale in an article in the October 1936 issue of *Yachting:*

Only when we were three hundred miles south-west of the Fastnet, scudding before another heavy blow, did we get a peep out of [the radio]: "A depression south-west of Ireland is moving rapidly toward the east. . . ." So were we.

It was this depression that dropped the barometer steadily at the rate of one millimeter [1.3 millibars] per hour for fifteen hours while the wind increased and the weather changed to the leaden dull gray of the Irish coast. By morning the seas had made up and, under a lowering sky, we ran before an angry sea, long cresting greybacks, a regular Fastnet sea. Under close reefed mainsail and storm jib, we raced before combers whose trough was as deep as our ship was long. Lifted high on the back of the back of a wave which rose mountain high behind us, we careened dizzily down its face in a fury of foam at the speed of a surfboard. As the wave overtook us, we were brought up sharply, and the water roared under our counter, leaving us wallowing sickeningly as the bow settled, burying the length of the ship in the next wave ahead. At this moment the ship, seemingly with no headway, felt as though she had given up struggling and might be dragged down by the forces opposing her. Then, recovering, she would shake the load of water from her decks and race before the next greyback.

It was anxious work at the tiller. Twice, curling breakers crashed over the stern, filling the decks and flooding the cockpit. But we were expecting them and were securely lashed in the cockpit. They did no harm except to fill a sea boot and once catch the companionway hatch partly open and send half a ton of water below.

The sun came out for a time to light up the wind-swept seascape. A vicious wind whipped the tops off the breaking waves in a thin cutting spray that stung like hail. We were making eight and a half to nine knots before it when the slides at the top of the mainsail started to go—the marlin seizing began to part. We lowered the mainsail to repair the slides, but soon found it unwise to attempt to reset it. The wind was probably up to force 10 and, under one hundred square feet of storm jib, we ran before it, making five knots. We tried our favorite raffee [a small squaresail], but the ship rolled her decks under and we took it in again. When the wind eased a bit, we set the staysail and drove on toward our landfall.

At dusk, on the twentieth day, we climbed the rigging and found three low black humps on the horizon to the north slightly more solid than the heaving sea around them. They were islands—the Scillies. As night fell, the flashing lights showed Bishop Rock astern and the Wolf [Rock] abeam. We were in the Channel.

Written in the classic narrative style of sea stories, Ames's account is of a boat heavier and slower than most of the yachts hit by the worst of the 1979 gale. Though *Hamburg* had her problems, neither she nor her crew was hurt. The seas the author described (and photographed for the article) were large and broke from time to time, but they do not seem to have been as inherently vicious as the waves that battered much of the Fastnet fleet. *Hamburg*'s waves were the seas that offshore sailors believe they can cope with. What most of the Fastnet sailors encountered were the nasty, curling breakers usually associated with a rocky lee shore or with the early-nineteenth-century sea battle paintings of J.M.W. Turner and Philip James de Loutherbourg, in which jawlike waves break through the cannon smoke to devour helpless sailors clinging to shattered spars.

In mid-August 1970, a depression took a path similar to the one taken by the 1979 cell, swinging over Ireland during the early hours on Sunday, August 16. It poured several inches of rain on England, causing severe flooding. Although the Fastnet race was not being sailed (it is a bienniel race sailed in odd-numbered years) several ocean races were under way. A fleet of boats between twenty and thirty feet in length was racing around the Isle of Wight, and six of the twenty-one starters withdrew when the gale quickly built. Only one boat required assistance—her rudder broke. The London *Times* boating correspondent, John Nicholls, described the race as "one of those events that will be talked about long after the rest of the season is forgotten." Meanwhile, several boats were missing in the Western Approaches. One, a Royal Navy yacht named *Temeraire*, became the focus of a search that included a helicopter, two frigates, a German ship, and two minesweepers. Twelve hours after she was reported missing, *Temeraire* was located and towed to port by the Penlee, Cornwall, lifeboat. One of her crew, Sublieutenant Tony Higham, was quoted by the *Times* as saying that "the seas were reaching the top of the mast—about thirty-five feet—certainly enough to overpower a small yacht."

While those descriptions confirm the belief that fierce storms are no novelty, they do not prove that bad weather always precisely repeats itself. This is so even in the same storm. An extraordinary aspect of the 1979 Fastnet gale is that while many survivors agreed to a considerable extent about the wind and sea conditions, some have entirely different accounts of what happened between early Tuesday morning and late Tuesday night. One is tempted to explain these differences with the

Taken forty-three years apart, these photographs show the waters of the Western Approaches in strong gale conditions.

*Above:* Looking astern from *Hamburg* during the 1936 transatlantic race in conditions that the photographer described as "a regular Fastnet sea."

*On the opposite page, above:* Having surfed down one wave, and having caught its crest at the back of their necks, Eric Swenson at the wheel of *Toscana,* with Stuart Woods (*left*) and Dale Cheek (*right*), prepare for the next sea beginning to rise behind them. Sherry Jagerson took this picture while clinging to the mast.

  *Below:* The author at the helm of *Toscana* on Tuesday morning as Susan Noyes and John Ruch endure the cold. *Toscana* was making nine and sometimes ten knots under forestaysail and triple-reefed mainsail.

*Ben Ames, Sherry Jagerson, and Nick Noyes*

Rashomon Premise, which is inspired by the Japanese film in which several different witnesses give varying accounts of a crime, each dependent upon the social and psychological perspective of the narrator. In this case, however, we are dealing with observable data that share a constant standard: the ease with which a boat was steered under a given spread of sail. By applying this standard and evaluating these stories, we may be able to judge whether or not the conditions were the same everywhere on the course in the Western Approaches.

*Toscana* rarely experienced a sea that was much more dangerous than the ones that had driven *Hamburg* during the force 10 gale forty-three years earlier. We kept going at near maximum speed and under excellent control, we were able to tack into the wind and around Fastnet Rock, and the two helmsmen, Eric Swenson and myself, were able to steer for hours without losing control of the wheel. As Eric wrote later, "It was a wrestling match, but one that was never in doubt." By comparison, the helmsmen of *Aries*, a forty-six-footer on the American Admiral's Cup team, at times could not hold the steering wheel. "The boat was totally out of control," her navigator, Dave Kilponen, remembered. *Aries* rounded Fastnet Rock just after midnight; by 2:00 A.M. Tuesday, she was swept by breaking waves about once every ten minutes. The farther east she sailed, the rougher the seas became. At 5:00 A.M., when she was about fifty miles east of the Rock, she was being swept once every minute. As she surfed down waves under storm jib alone, Kilponen said, "the rudder started with a low vibration and ended up a jet engine whine." The mast shook so violently that a running backstay fell off and a spreader cracked.

*Aries* was a type of boat different from *Toscana*, light, shallow, and tricky to sail well. Yet a boat about five hours ahead of her that was very similar in concept to *Toscana* was having her difficulties, too. This yacht was *Tenacious*, a sixty-one-footer owned by the flamboyant American Ted Turner.

*Tenacious* rounded Fastnet Rock at 6:30 Monday evening. Assuming that she averaged nine knots as she sailed close-hauled and then reached toward the Isles of Scilly, she was approximately ninety-five miles down the course at 5:00 A.M., when *Aries*'s worst troubles started and when *Toscana* turned the Rock. At about that time, when *Toscana* was beating to windward over the last few miles under triple-reefed mainsail and forestaysail in about fifty knots of wind, *Tenacious*—thirteen feet longer, more stable, and more buoyant—was reaching across at least sixty knots of wind under number-4 jib alone. Turner had ordered the mainsail lowered just after midnight. Even under this small rig she suffered knockdowns. Once she was badly rolled while her navigator, Peter Bowker, was on deck trying to fix her position with a portable radio direction finder. Bowker, who was not wearing a safety harness, was thrown heavily against the helmsman, Jim Mattingly, and their combined force dented the stainless-steel steering wheel. Gary Jobson, a watch captain in *Tenacious* since 1977, noticed that for the first time in his experience she was leaking.

When the wind veered into the north-west and came directly over the big white sloop's transom, Turner's crew set the number-4 jib and the reaching jib "wing and wing"—one trimmed to port, the other trimmed to starboard, and each held steady by a spinnaker pole that was secured to the mast. This is the classic rig for running before strong winds; boats of all sizes have sailed for weeks on end like this, dead before the wind and easily steered, since the sideways forces on the two sails tend to balance out. It is an illegal rig for racing if the mainsail is also carried. *Tenacious* ran this way for a period of at least two hours, according to Greg Shires, who was in her crew. Meanwhile, many other boats were difficult to steer until their skippers sailed a safer and longer course ten or twenty degrees to windward of a dead run. (*Tenacious* eventually won the race with best corrected time.)

If *Toscana* had been sailing near *Tenacious*, I doubt if we would have been able to carry more sail area than the larger boat

---

OVERLEAF: Ted Turner's *Tenacious*, a sixty-one-footer, was near the area of greatest distress. During one roll, her navigator was thrown into her helmsman and the steering wheel was dented. *Tenacious* eventually won the race on corrected time. *Barry Pickthall*

did. Designed by the same man, Olin Stephens, and with approximately the same shape and proportions, the two boats probably behave similarily in rough weather, which is a way of saying that the conditions in which they were sailing were strikingly different.

Another big American boat, *Boomerang*, a sixty-four-footer owned by George Coumentaros, rounded Fastnet Rock about three hours behind *Tenacious*. When the force 10 gale swept in, her crew shortened sail until they flew only the number-4 jib— the next smallest to the forestaysail and the storm jib. At 8:00 A.M. the wind increased. The crew set the forestaysail and, during a bad knockdown, cut the sheets, halyard, and tack on the number-4 jib, allowing the sail to blow away to leeward. The waves built until, under forestaysail alone, the big yacht began surfing wildly at enormous speeds, once registering 24.6 knots on her speedometer. A major problem was avoiding other yachts. "We set a careful watch for smaller boats laboring in the troughs of waves as we raced down the crests," a *Boomerang* crew member, Jeff Neuberth, wrote in *Yachting* after the race. "Avoiding collision was of paramount concern. We passed twenty to thirty boats with either bare poles and a skeleton crew or no crew on deck at all, and several boats hove-to with minimal canvas set. . . . The rescue helicopters, the spotter planes, and the radio traffic all indicated to us that the smallest boats were really having a rough go of it. The radio traffic to and from the *Overijssel* and the number of helicopters in the area indicated that the severity of the wind and sea were getting to the smaller boats." The gale could also have been getting to the larger boats, but Neuberth, like many crew members in big boats that day, clearly had faith in his own vessel if only because of her size. If *Boomerang* was close enough to the area of greater problems to see the rescue helicopters and hear the guard ship's radio transmissions, then the wind and sea that were driving her to such great speeds under so little sail must also have been experienced by the boats in distress. She was roughly one hundred miles down the course at 8:00 A.M. Fifty miles to the north-west, *Toscana's* anemometer showed a steady fifty to fifty-five knots, and under considerably more sail than *Boomerang* was carrying, we rarely reached speeds higher than ten knots as we surfed down long, high, and manageable waves.

Another big boat ahead of *Toscana* was *Siska*, a lightweight seventy-seven-footer owned by an Australian, Rolly Tasker. "I've never seen anything worse, and I've sailed in fifty-five knots before," one of her crew members, Gerry McGarry, told a reporter from the *Sydney Morning Herald*. "The tops of the waves were breaking and toppling over in the wind. We could imagine what they could do to a small boat. We continued racing, but it was survival conditions, really. . . . Our thoughts were for the little boats when we started getting distress calls. We were kept busy relaying the calls." As if to prove—despite the laws of proportion and the confidence of their crews—that even large boats were not immune from the gale, *Siska*'s boom broke as the wind died, and she finished the race with her mainsail awkwardly trimmed.

Meanwhile, the small yachts on which everybody was expending so much concern were coping with the gale with various degrees of success. Three or four hours ahead of *Toscana*, fast boats like *Imp* and *Eclipse* reached along under mainsail or small jib alone. Many crews later said that they would have preferred to set storm trysails, but because the race regulations had not required them, the weight-conscious crews had not brought these small sails along. With jibs set alone, way forward on the bow, many boats were unbalanced and difficult to steer. The helmsmen had to work hard to stay on course and to avoid broaching. In *Toscana*, more able to carry sail, our triple-reefed mainsail and the forestaysail were set so closely together that the center of pressure of the wind on the sails was almost directly above the center of pressure of the water on the hull. Steering the unbalanced boats was like driving a car with poor shock absorbers and a back trunk full of sandbags: the front end is light, the back end is heavy, and on every sway to one side the car wants to steer to the other side. In both cars and boats, imbalance demands extremely careful steering if the vehicle is to stay on course. Steering the better balanced *Toscana*

After their carbon fiber rudder snapped, the crew of *Casse Tete V* steers using a spin-naker pole as a rudder, as big seas still run. *Ambrose Greenway*

was like driving a well-tuned car in which the weight is evenly distributed. Control was positive and relatively untiring.

Whether or not they were unbalanced, an enormous number of boats went out of control in the seas. The postrace inquiry conducted jointly by the Royal Ocean Racing Club and the Royal Yachting Association included a questionnaire sent to all Fastnet race boats in which the skippers were asked if they were knocked down to horizontal or almost horizontal (90 degrees) and beyond horizontal (including a 360-degree roll). Of the 235 skippers who responded to the questionnaire, fully 113 (or 48 percent) said their boats had been knocked down to horizontal or almost horizontal. Amazingly, 77 skippers (or 33 percent) said they had been rolled over. In other words, 25 percent of the entire 303-boat Fastnet race fleet capsized entirely—the equivalent of one-quarter of all cars in the Indianapolis 500 crashing. In the accounts of the handful of previous capsizings of individual boats—off Cape Horn, or in Atlantic storms—the point has usually been made that the crews were extremely lucky to have survived. That the calamity occurred to so many boats in a single twenty-hour period is mind-numbering evidence of extraordinary conditions.

A boat that runs before a gale at too great a speed may capsize by going too fast down the face of a wave, pushing her bow into the back of the wave ahead, and pitchpoling over her bow onto her deck. More likely, she may broach (heel to one side and suddenly head in the other direction) on the face of one wave, end up with her side to the waves, and then be smashed amidships by several tons of water breaking off the following wave. If sailing too slowly, she may be overtaken and "pooped" by a wave that breaks over her stern and into her cockpit. Such a breaker could swamp her and eventually roll her over. Lying a-hull, at about thirty degrees to the direction of the waves with no speed on, is thought by many sailors to be the best way to avoid pitchpoling, rolling, and pooping. But in massively breaking seaways, the boat may be even more vulnerable lying a-hull than she would be running before it under control or heaving-to—working slowly across the seas under a storm sail.

*Police Car*, a lightweight forty-two-foot boat on the Austra-

lian Admiral's Cup team, was three times knocked over to about
120 degrees, putting her mast in the water, while running before it at what her crew thought was a safe speed of five or six
knots. Apparently, she was going too slowly to allow the helmsmen to steer around bad waves. Her crew recognized the problem and increased her average speed to about eight knots by
changing the trim of her storm jib (the only sail they had up,
since even with four reefs the mainsail was too big; her owner
had not brought a storm trysail). She sometimes surfed down
waves at much higher speeds, and her helmsmen had to be alert
to any bad waves that might come along or that they might plow
into. Chris Bouzaid, an experienced ocean-racing sailor, was a
helmsman in *Police Car;* later, he described the conditions in an
article in *Yachting:*

". . . Every sea was different. Some of them we would
square away and run down the front of. Others were just far too
steep to do this. One imagines a sea to be a long sausagelike
piece of water moving across the ocean. However, this was not
the case at all as these seas had too many breaks in them and
were not uniform. We found that in many cases we could pick
our way through the seas, finding a little valley between seas
and ducking through, now that we had more boat speed. Once
we got all of this together, we had very little trouble. We found
that we were managing to avoid all the breaking seas, either by
cutting through the sea and going beyond the breaks, or bearing
away on the sea prior to the break to avoid having it hit the boat.
During the next four hours, we were in fact only hit once by a
breaking sea, and that was only because the helmsman (me) was
talking to the other crew members and not concentrating on the
job at hand." Unfortunately, few helmsmen of Fastnet race
boats were as skillful and knowledgeable as Bouzaid.

Another vivid description of the sea was written for private

---

*Police Car,* a light, well-sailed forty-two-footer on the winning Australian Admiral's Cup
team, was rolled down several times before her crew discovered that making her go
faster also made her more seaworthy. Like many boats, she did not carry a storm trysail;
like many crews, they wished they had. *William Payne*

circulation by John Ellis, owner of the thirty-two-footer *Kate*.
While his estimates of wind strength and wave height were conservative compared with those of other Fastnet race survivors—
the wind, he thought, rarely got over fifty knots and "by no
stretch of the imagination could the seas have been higher than
twenty-five feet"—Ellis shared in Bouzaid's belief that the shape
of the waves determined their effects:

The frequency was much too short for comfort, giving steep wall-sided
seas, streaked heavily with foam and breaking (at worst) in the top six
feet. More usually, the top three to four feet would break. What
seemed to happen was that three or four seas would build up into a suc-
cession of breakers, although these would not break along their whole
length but in isolated cusps which, having broken along their length,
would then break outwards behind the fast-moving crest in a sort of
saucer of outward-breaking crestlets. At no stage did we see the force
11–12 type of spume (which we have read about but not seen) which is
said to turn the whole sea surface into one coherent, blinding sheet of
wind-borne spray.

Looking downwind, one could see the wave trains forming and dis-
sipating in moderate order with, occasionally, the odd monster hump-
ing its back well above the average height—say another six feet. The
occurrence of these was, as we say, occasional but not unusual and they
were responsible for the number of poopings which we experienced.
Turning to this phenomenon for a moment, let us confess that we could
not, of course, hold our heading of 20 degrees with precision. Normally, we could hold this between 10 degrees and 30 degrees. The
total maximum swing was more like 360 degrees to 45 degrees, when
hit by breakers. The poopings occurred when we were close to the 45-
degree heading, with a breaking sea closing. The helmsman would
hear, but not see, the breaker coming: it would break cleanly up the
retroussé transom . . . over the helmsman and his relief, into the cockpit, up over the washboard and hatch, and plane on over the ship, leaving cleanly by the bow.

*Kate*'s experienced crew gave up racing at 4:00 A.M. on Tuesday, when she was about ninety miles from the Rock. They
threw over lines and doused all sails. Her owner concluded that
she survived at least partly because they kept her speed low. By
10:00 A.M., he wrote, "it was beginning to be borne in upon us
that we should come to no harm. Indeed, the owner confesses

that during the afternoon watch, he found himself chanting inspiring songs at the wheel, exhilaration having succeeded apprehension."

Many of the most frightening—in fact murderous—events happened within forty miles of *Kate* and *Boomerang*. Heading east in this area were *Tenacious, Acadia,* and *Police Car*. Trying to head west were *Grimalkin, Trophy, Windswept,* and possibly Major Maclean in *Fluter*. When the coastguards compiled their report on the search and rescue operations conducted by the helicopters, they provided twenty estimated positions of boats and equipment that were located, aided, or retrieved on August 14, 15, and 16. While the positions are not entirely reliable, if only because the pilots were extremely busy with rescue efforts, the trend is clear: most of the distress seen by the helicopter crews took place within a circle with a diameter of forty miles whose center was at 50° 42' north and 7° 14' west—a point seventy miles west-north-west of Land's End, one hundred miles south-south-east of Fastnet Rock, and ten miles north of the rhumb line, or direct course, between the two landmarks. All of the boats located by the helicopters in this forty-mile circle were smaller than thirty-five feet in length. (See Appendix III.)

After the race, many would claim that smaller boats suffered the greatest damage simply because they were smaller boats. This argument was especially popular among crews in large yachts who neglected to see that boats such as *Tenacious, Acadia,* and *Boomerang*—each longer than fifty feet——experienced severe difficulties in the same general area. What was special about this area of the Western Approaches was not only that it was filled with small boats but that it was also overflowing with especially strong gusts and dangerous seas. Sixty miles to the north-west, we in *Toscana* experienced nowhere near the same extremely violent conditions. Only by sheer bad luck did so many small boats find themselves in this area, more than ten hours from shore, just as the gale swept through.

Weather can behave in strange and mysterious ways; calms and storms may be small and localized or they may cover entire oceans. Atmospheric pressure, surface and submarine land formations, and the spin of the earth can combine to create storms out of calms and maelstroms out of millponds. One part of a body of water may be safe while another is lethal. What usually makes the difference is the size and shape of the waves.

Waves often are compared with the motions of a rope secured at one end and moved up and down at the other end at a steady speed. Crests and troughs will migrate from one end to the other in a rhythmic, predictable pattern. The fibers in the rope may stretch, but they do not move. Similarly, the water at the surface of waves does not move markedly in the direction toward which the waves roll (the surface water does, however, rotate in small circular orbits, forward on the crest and backward in the trough). The length of the rope and the strength of the person moving the free end determine the height, shape, and length (distance between the crests) of the man-made waves.

The size and shape of water waves depend upon several factors: the strength of the wind, the amount of time that the wind blows from a given direction, the fetch (or distance over which the wind blows), the depth of the water, and the direction and strength of currents. Through observation and experiment, oceanographers have developed mathematical tables that can help in the prediction of wave height and length. For example, a twenty-knot wind that blows over a fetch of one hundred nautical miles of deep water for twelve hours will generate waves whose maximum height is six feet and whose length is two hundred feet, and which travel at a speed of more than twenty knots. A forty-knot wind with the same fetch and blowing for the same length of time will generate waves as large as *thirty* feet, with a length of six hundred feet and a speed of more than thirty-five knots. (The reason why wave size increases by a factor of five while the wind speed merely doubles is that the wind's *force* is directly proportional to the square of the wind speed.) As the wind dies, so do the waves, but at a much slower rate.

When waves encounter contrary currents, they increase in size by large factors. The Scripps Institute of Oceanography, in California, estimates that wave height may be doubled by a contrary current of only two or three knots. Likewise, waves increase in height when they pass over shoal water, and changes in the contour of the sea bed, even in relatively deep water, may affect the height of waves. As the height increases, a wave may steepen to the point where the base can no longer support the top, and the wave collapses on itself and becomes a breaker. The pile of white water that falls off the top of a breaking wave may be accelerated by the wind that created the wave to begin with.

A type of wave that all seamen fear is the rogue wave, which angles across the train of normal seas and sometimes collides with one to create a breaker. The oceanographer William G. Van Dorn writes in his book *Oceanography and Seamanship* that 5 percent of deep sea waves are abnormally high "rogues." They may be caused by distant winds of a force and direction different from the local wind or by some other special circumstance. Usually, these rogue waves pass by vessels with little effect. Judging from the reports of the sailors caught toward the middle of the Western Approaches during the Fastnet storm, rogue waves were more the norm there than the exception.

Mathematics were working against the Fastnet race crews. On the top of the long south-west groundswell was one set of waves created by the force 6 south wind that blew all Monday afternoon, plus a second set pushed up by the force 9 and 10 south-west gale that blew from 11:00 P.M. Monday until about 5:00 A.M. Tuesday. When the wind continued to strengthen and veer as the depression passed to the north, the first two sets remained, and by 9:00 A.M. Tuesday there was a third set of waves running in from the north-west. As each set of waves aged, it increased in height and speeded up, so by midmorning Tuesday there was a great clash of ten-, twenty-, and perhaps even forty-foot waves from many directions, creating a sea of breakers.

The depression itself may have contributed to the roughness of the seas. As the fast-moving deepening low (bringing on the fourth lowest barometric pressure for a British August since 1900) sped across the Approaches, it created a mound of water under its center. Before this mound was a surge that, like a big wave, pushed east, creating currents that swirled around the depression and perhaps turned back against the wind. Saltwater people tend to believe that current is caused only by the tide, but on the huge nontidal Great Lakes of North America, one- and two-knot currents called seiches are created in the surge of water ahead of moving depressions. On the lakes these currents can conspire with gale-force winds to create mammoth seas that have been known to swallow up freighters and tankers. The same phenomenon may have occurred in the bay-like Western Approaches during the Fastnet gale. In addition, wind can create a current on any body of water—as much as half a knot in a force 6 wind blowing for twelve hours.

The veer in wind direction and in the direction of currents caused by the depression was particularly sudden in the southern part of the low-pressure cell, where the storm had changed its shape from that of a rough circle to a teardrop. A trough of low pressure ran from north to south down the center of this teardrop, and where the trough was deepest, the angle between the contour lines of atmospheric pressure was greatest. Since wind direction tends to be roughly parallel to the gradient lines (actually, angled in at about fifteen degrees around a depression), the wind shift at this point was more sudden than it was at the more gradual turns in the lines of equal air pressure. As well, the wind probably blew strongest in the trough. Directly in the path of this moving line of suddenly veering wind were the boats in the middle of the Western Approaches. Because the wind veer was abrupt, the angle between the old and the new waves was sharp—as much as forty-five degrees.

Apparently, the worst disturbance caused by the depression was relatively local. Later on Tuesday, when the storm swept across southern Scotland, it kicked up waves large enough to force the cancellation of the Hull to Rotterdam ferry on which several horses in the British show jumping team were booked ("Heavy seas delay British horses," ran a headline in Thursday's *Daily Telegraph*), while, 125 miles to the south, the Harwich to Hook of Holland ferry ran on schedule.

There is other evidence that the storm was more violent near

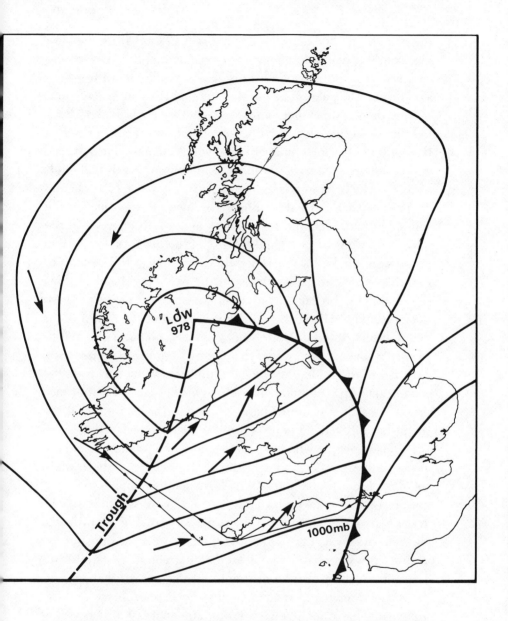

**Low**
**978**

**Trough**

**1000mb**

A synoptic chart of Low Y at 7:00 A.M. (British Summer Time) on Tuesday, August 14. The drastic wind shift in the trough was probably a major cause of the dangerous seas in the middle of the Western Approaches.

the rhumb line between Land's End and Fastnet Rock than farther south. A man from Houston, Texas, named Bill Wallace was
completing a single-handed transatlantic voyage in a thirty-foot
sloop when the gale broke on Monday night. By his calculation,
he was then seventy-five miles west-south-west of Bishop Rock
lighthouse in the Isles of Scilly, and about ninety miles south of
the center of the forty-mile circle in which so many Fastnet race
yachts suffered damage. Wallace told the company that built
his boat (which summarized his report in a news release) that he
experienced no major difficulties. He lowered the sails, set the
self-steerer to keep the boat at an angle of 30 degrees to the
wind, and went below. Unlike many of the boats that lay a-hull
at the same angle, his was rolled down only once, to 120 degrees
("And I've got the coffee stains on the cabin overhead to show
it"), and flying tin cans cut his scalp. Solid water never came on
deck or below. His boat, an American design called the J-30, is
not radically different from boats such as *Grimalkin* and *Windswept*. Wallace also reported that the night never darkened. "By
nightfall in the middle of the gale, the stars were out, then the
moon came up," he said. The only light that many Fastnet race
crews saw was that from a flare, and we in *Toscana* enjoyed the
moon for only half an hour before the blackness closed back in.
(Like many people who were on the sidelines, Wallace could not
resist the temptation to judge the Fastnet crews. "There was a
lot of panic out there," he said. "Those people racing haven't encountered the ocean and what it can be like. Most of them have
just been sailing around bays and harbors." What he probably
did not know was that, whatever their experience, most of the
racing crews probably faced exceptional conditions quite different from those that he encountered that same night.)

A problematical explanation for the extraordinary seas in-
volves a bank of relatively shallow water that lay in the path of
the trough of low atmospheric pressure and its violent winds.
Called the Labadie Bank, it is about ten miles south of the
Land's End to Fastnet Rock rhumb line and is also near the
forty-mile circle. This relatively shoal area has depths of between twenty-one and fifty fathoms and averages about forty

fathoms (a fathom is six feet). The water in the Western Approaches is by no means deep, since it lies over the European Continental Shelf and has an average depth of about sixty fathoms. Although oceanographers have argued that a difference in depth of twenty fathoms so far under the surface is not significant enough to cause especially bad waves, the Labadie Bank has earned a reputation for rough water among the fishermen who frequent it.

At least one yachtsman has agreed with the fishermen. During the 1931 Fastnet race, the fifty-one-footer *Maitenes II* was swept over the Labadie Bank in a rapidly veering force 9 to force 10 gale much like the 1979 storm. Her skipper, Commander W. B. Luard, Royal Navy (Retired), later devoted a chapter in his book *Where the Tides Meet* to the race and the storm.

"Had we been in open waters," he wrote, "she would have lain, as she wished, under bare poles with absolute safety; but the steepness and the irregularity of the breaking seas made it essential, in my opinion, to keep her bow or stern to them at all costs." A drogue was thrown over the stern to slow her down, and the crew began to pour fish oil into the sea to attempt to flatten the waves, an accepted storm tactic. It was at this point that Colonel C.H. Hudson was washed overboard while adjusting one of the oil bags. He grabbed the line to the drogue, but it was torn from his hands and, weighed down by foul-weather gear and boots, he sank.

As she drifted east at six knots, *Maitenes* experienced increasingly vicious seas that occasionally came over the stern and pooped her. The crew, demoralized by the loss of the colonel and exhausted by their efforts, sighted a trawler and sent a message by semaphore requesting that it stand by until the gale moderated, when they could be taken off. "I estimated we were then approximately eighty miles south-east (magnetic) of Fastnet Rock," Luard wrote. He went on:

"About an hour later, wind and sea having again increased, I semaphored that we could no longer run with safety if the weather became any worse, and the trawler replied that she had just received another gale warning. The seas now changed in character—we were on the Labadie Bank—became still steeper, still more confused and irregular, running in from all sides; and we were pooped heavily several times. Though the glass [barometer] had just started to rise it seemed likely, in view of the renewed gale warning, that it would blow harder than before from west and north-west and drive us onto a lee shore in less than eighteen hours, with, as likely as not, the trawler standing by unable to be of any assistance. On the other hand, it seemed possible that the gale might moderate in time to let us heave-to again on the starboard tack and work clear [of the Cornish coast]. I realized, however, that the ship [*Maitenes*] was in imminent danger of being fatally pooped, and after considering the situation from every point of view, I concluded that I was not justified in taking further risks."

Luard fired off flares, and after great effort and some damage to the yacht and the destruction of the trawler's dory, some fishermen came aboard. As "the ship was clearing the bank, the seas became more regular, and soon the wind started easing." The next morning, *Maitenes* was taken in tow for Swansea.

"*Maitenes* is a magnificent sea boat," Luard concluded. "Had we not been driven over the Labadie Bank all would have been well, and had we been off soundings [in the open ocean] there would have been no cause for anxiety; for she could have been left to her own devices, if overpowered by the weight of wind, or been put before the seas and allowed to run with perfect safety. . . . The sea this year was the steepest I have yet seen, often too steep for any boat to rise to; but it seemed, at times, as though the drogue tended to keep her stern from lifting freely. . . . I have come to the conclusion that if caught in a similar sea again I should not attempt to reduce a ship's speed as much as possible, nor keep her running at full speed . . . but aim at striking a happy medium."

Thus did Luard unknowingly anticipate the seamanship problems that so challenged the men and women who raced over the same waters many years later. He ended his account with a warning: "Granted that identical conditions would not be met once again in a thousand times, but it is the thousandth chance that may lead, alas, to tragedy and disaster."

So strongly did Luard believe that the Labadie Bank was important in the creation of bad seas in the Western Approaches that he did not try to explain exactly how such a deep shoal could have such a great effect. Oceanographers might challenge his assumption as another fishermen's superstition, and it is true that fishermen—or at least the English and French fishermen with whom I have talked—fear the bank in bad weather. It is also true that *Maitenes II* and many boats in the 1979 Fastnet race confronted increasingly dangerous seas as they approached the area of the bank. There is no question that the real culprit in both storms was the rapidly shifting force 10 to force 12 wind, which in 1979 veered through 135 degrees, from south to north-west, in a little more than twelve hours. Perhaps the Labadie Bank was disrupting an already confused sea just enough to turn it into a mess of "the most fearsome things." Or the immense variety of winds, waves, surges of water, and currents created by the deep, fast-moving storm could have focused all their energies on the area of water that lay approximately one hundred miles south-south-east of Fastnet Rock.

Whatever the cause of the seaway, there is no doubt about its effects, and, despite the convictions of Commander Luard and several of the survivors of the 1979 storm that they had finally figured out how to survive in those waves, no single storm tactic was a guarantee against disaster. Hilaire Belloc once wrote, "The sea drives truth into a man like salt." The truth here is that there are occasions when men can do little or nothing to help themselves.

# 7 The Rescuers: Asking the Impossible

EVER SINCE NOAH, the sea has been a symbol of both salvation and destruction. When Jonah escaped to it, the sea, acting as an agent of God's wrath, almost killed him. After parting for Moses, it drowned the Egyptians. Noah's flood, in fact, is not unique. Among the flood myths of other cultures is that of the pre-Columbian Aztec Indians of Mexico, whose calendar stone depicted three ages of progress leading to a fourth age of destruction. In this fourth age, as Joseph Campbell writes in *The Mythic Image*, "water, gentle mothering vehicle of the energies of birth, nourishment, and growth, became a deluge." Western man has learned to use the sea for pleasure, and fear of the sea's violence may have become less conscious than faith in its powers of regeneration.

The people of the west of England are not so sanguine. An English folk tale relates how the sea off the north coast of Cornwall calls for its victims. One calm night, "when all was still save the monotonous fall of the light waves upon the sand," a seaman—a fisherman, perhaps, or a pilot—took a walk on a Cornish beach near Porth. A voice came to him from the Western Approaches: "The hour is come, but not the man," the voice said, and repeated the strange message three times. Looking inland, the seaman saw a dark humanlike figure standing on the top of a nearby hill. The figure paused for a moment, and then rushed down the hill and across the beach, and disappeared into the sea.

Lured by fate, profit, or pleasure, men have been rushing down the hills into English waters for centuries, and not all of them have survived. The sea is a common denominator for ev-

---

The lifeboat *Guy and Claire Hunter,* from St. Mary's, Scilly Isles, in the Western Approaches on Tuesday afternoon. She escorted two boats to port and towed *Festina Tertia* (which had lost one man) and her surviving crew of six to St. Mary's. *Royal Navy*

erybody who lives on the British Isles. Its attractions are represented by a popular BBC television show in which a pleasantly
inquisitive man named John Noakes travels Britain in his small
ketch, seeking out interesting people. (By contrast, in an American version of *Go with Noakes*, Charles Kuralt traveled in a mammoth, gas-inhaling camper.) Lifeboat stations are listed along
with fire departments on pages devoted to emergency telephone
numbers in local directories. Until quite recently, shipwreck
and drowning on a massive scale were an accepted part of British
life. In 1864, 1,741 ships and 516 lives were lost around the
coastline of the United Kingdom; in 1880, 1,303 ships and 2,100
lives; in 1909, 733 ships and 4,738 lives. As the ships decreased
in number, they increased in size, so every wreck killed more
people than the previous one. On one day in 1859, 195 ships
sank or were wrecked. During November 1893, 298 ships foundered.

    One of the very worst places for wrecks is the eighty-square-
mile archipelago of the Isles of Scilly, twenty-eight miles off
Land's End and almost that distance out in the Western Approaches. Gales there are bad and frequent, currents are confused, seas are wild. Until the mid-nineteenth century there was
no lighthouse to protect seamen from the chain's west and south
sides, and ships searching for the Channel or the Approaches
often ran aground there. Constructed on a rock not much larger
than a wide boulder, Bishop's Rock lighthouse now towers over
the islands; sometimes, the spray from breaking waves seems
to tower even higher. Now guarded on the south-west by the
Bishop, on the north by Round Island light, and on the east by
Wolf Rock and St. Mary's lights, the fifty-odd islands and islets
and many rocks of the Scilly Isles are still not much less dangerous now than they were in the 1860s, when they and other landmarks in the Land's End area accounted for the loss of 394 ships,
or in 1875, when 335 people died after the ocean liner *Schiller*
foundered on the Retarrier Ledges. It was on the Seven Stones
rocks off the Scilles that the tanker *Torrey Canyon* split apart in
1967, spilling a life-threatening amount of oil into the clear waters and onto sandy beaches in Cornwall, Devon, and Brittany

That no oil fouled the Isles of Scilly is not really surprising. The lucky, semitropical islands have, like the sea around them, been a haven as well as a danger since they were first settled about 3000 B.C. A reflection of this security is one of the charges brought against Thomas Seymour in 1549, when his aspirations to gain control of the crown became known. He was accused of buying "the strong and dangerous Isles of Scilly" and conspiring with pirates to use them as a refuge "if anything for his demerits should be attempted against him." Scillonians (as the islanders call themselves; they are *not* Cornishmen) have always made excellent use of the chain's isolation and natural strengths, first in Bronze Age tribes, then in medieval religious orders seeking privacy, next in fishing communities, and now in tourist associations.

Throughout, the Scillonians, like island people everywhere, have willingly accepted what the sea has provided for them, and among those gifts have been wrecked ships. From the days when church services were ended at the arrival of news of fresh wrecks, salvaging has been an important part of Scilly life. A man could win a healthy part of a year's income during a few hours of dangerous, wet work helping to salvage a stranded vessel or her cargo.

Today, wrecking remains important but in different ways. Divers, primarily from the mainland, have found treasure in and around the wrecks of four Royal Navy ships, including HMS *Association*, that were blown by gales onto rocks in 1707, with a loss of almost two thousand men. Other divers have searched for vases and paintings belonging to Sir William Hamilton, the husband of Horatio Nelson's Emma, which were lost when the *Colossus* sank in 1798. There are others: the *Hollandia*, whose recovered treasure brought nearly £100,000 in auction; the *Princess Maria;* and some 540 other wrecks lying within eight miles of the islands.

Competing with this revival of the salvage business is a small wrecks artifacts industry. A family named Gibson has photographed Cornish and Scilly wrecks since the 1860s, and their shop in Hugh Town, on the chain's main island, St. Mary's, is

wallpapered with dramatic, gruesome pictures that are for sale
at £1.50. Gibson photographs illustrate at least four books on
Scilly wrecks. And on the nearby island of Trescoe, figureheads,
trailboards, and other ornaments from wrecks are on display in
the aptly named Valhalla Maritime Museum.

While their survival has been dependent upon opportunities
provided by visitors, both intended and accidental, Scillonians
are warmly generous people. Perhaps their good-heartedness
and sympathy toward people in trouble is an admission of their
own vulnerability. One Saturday a few months after the Fastnet
gale, a "jumble," or bake sale, was held in the tiny schoolhouse
on Trescoe Island, on which the famous gardens flourish. The
beneficiaries were the Cambodian refugees, whose horrible conditions had just become widely publicized. Children contributed toys, and adults brought pies and jams to the sale. The
winter population on the island is not much more than a
hundred people, including children, and is not wealthy, yet the
sale raised £50.

Two miles and a rough thirty-minute boat ride away in Hugh
Town, the Scillies' metropolis with perhaps five hundred year-
round residents, stands the great symbol of the Scillonians' gen-
erosity of spirit—the boathouse in which rested their lifeboat,
the *Guy and Claire Hunter*. There has been a volunteer lifeboat
station on St. Mary's continuously since 1874. The island's lifeboat crews had, by November 1979, rescued 627 survivors of
founderings.

Scillonians are not the only people to care about saving lives
at sea: in Great Britain and Ireland there exist more than two
hundred and fifty stations of the Royal National Life-boat Institution, over half of them on year-round duty with boats designed to withstand force 10 and stronger gales in open water.
The RNLI was formed in 1824, during the first great boom of
commercial sail. As ships increased in number, so too did shipwrecks and loss of life. Acting partly out of the humanitarianism
that seemed to strengthen in England along with commerce and
the empire, and partly out of fascination with the technical challenge of designing safe boats for difficult conditions, a wealthy

idealist named Sir William Hillary founded what was then called the National Institution for the Preservation of Life from Shipwreck. Among the institution's original policies that survive are rules that it be supported by donations; that widows and children of lifeboatmen who die in service be provided for; that special gallantry be recognized with awards; and that, regardless of nationality, any person in distress be attended to.

It took a while for this internationalist, humanitarian organization to gain popular attention. The cause received a boost in 1838 after the exploits of Grace Darling were widely publicized. A lighthouse keeper's daughter living in the Farne Islands, in north-east England, she helped her father rescue five people stranded on a wrecked paddle steamer. Fifty-four people were lost in the wreck. The contrast between the tragedy and the unassuming twenty-two-year-old heroine stimulated immense public interest in lifesaving. (Grace Darling died of tuberculosis four years later.)

As it grew, and as its vessels developed from rowboats to sailing gigs to the massive forty- to fifty-five-foot twin-screw power vessels in use today, the RNLI evolved into a large organization that stood above politics and dispute. The only large American institution even remotely like it is the Red Cross, except that the Red Cross is so ubiquitous in American life that it is all but taken for granted. Nobody takes the lifeboats for granted. On almost every shop counter in England, near the shore or inland, stands a small piggy bank with the shape of a lifeboat. Daily newspapers report lifeboat services (rescue efforts), whether successful or not, in the most respectful language. Sir Winston Churchill's patriotic words about the typical lifeboat summarize the universally held belief that its crews are somehow superhuman: "It drives on with a mercy which does not quail in the presence of death, it drives on as a proof, a symbol, a testimony, that man is created in the image of God, and that virtue and valor have not perished from the British race."

Whether the ten thousand or so lifeboatmen actually believe everything that is said about them is doubtful; many if not most of them are but fishermen in small communities, and the burden of personifying such an institution can be heavy. In any case, few are singled out for national attention, and the head office of the RNLI usually exerts little control over a station's activities. For most lifeboatmen, the local station *is* the RNLI, and although headquarters in Poole allots them funds and equipment and periodically inspects their boats, they feel beholden to nobody except themselves. Ask a lifeboat coxswain, or skipper, how many people his boat has saved and he will point to a plaque that details every service that his station has performed. Ask him how many have been saved in the history of the RNLI, and he probably will shrug his shoulders. (The answer, provided by the organization's headquarters, is about ninety-five thousand people.)

When the 1979 Fastnet storm struck, the coxswain of the St. Mary's lifeboat was, and had been since 1955, Matthew Lethbridge. He succeeded his father as cox, and his father succeeded *his* father. The three Lethbridges had commanded the St. Mary's lifeboat for 80 of the 123 years that there had been a station on the island. (The station was founded in 1837, abandoned in 1855, and revived in 1874.) A small, wiry man in his mid-fifties, Lethbridge was one of the few fishermen in Hugh Town who worked his traps and nets alone. He lived in a small row house with his wife and daughter, fished, mended his traps in the off-season, and waited for the call that, he knew, eventually would come from the coastguards to the station's secretary, and then to him. The records that he kept with white paint and brush on black plaques in the boathouse testified to his activities. In some years, the *Guy and Claire Hunter* was called out ten or twelve times; in other years, she and her eight-man crew went out less frequently. Unless there was a service, they were required to go on a test run every two months, and once a year an inspector came down from RNLI headquarters to look the boat over.

Sometimes when they went out, the crew had little more to

do than to tow a disabled yacht through the maze of unmarked rocks that protects Hugh Town's harbor. At other times, though, there was serious lifesaving work. In 1955, his first year as cox, the institution awarded Matt Lethbridge a bronze medal, its third-highest award for gallantry, for his efforts in rescuing a crew of twenty-five from a Panamanian steamer. Twelve years later, the boat took twenty-two men off the *Torrey Canyon*. Also in 1967, he was awarded a silver medal (the second-highest award) and his second in command and the boat's engineer received bronze medals for rescuing nineteen people from a large German power yacht and towing her to safety during a gale—a twenty-seven-hour service. Subsequent silver medals came three and nine years later.

Lethbridge's grandfather had taken the then Prince of Wales (later the Duke of Windsor) out in a lifeboat, and he himself had shown the present Prince of Wales around the *Guy and Claire Hunter* during one of the Prince's visits to St. Mary's. "We've been out in the *Britannia*, Pat and me," Lethbridge has said proudly, nodding to his wife. Perhaps it was the only way the Queen could have met him, since Lethbridge had visited the mainland only three times in thirty years, and on one of those occasions, when he went to London in 1976 to receive the British Empire Medal, the Queen was unable to award the medal personally.

Except for the few times when he endured London, Matt Lethbridge had never been away from the sea. During World War II, he served in Royal Air Force search and rescue boats, and returning to St. Mary's, he stepped directly into the lifeboat under his father's command. The second coxswain then was his uncle James; his brothers Harry and Richard now served in his own crew. In 1979, however, the family tradition was about to end, since Matt Lethbridge had no son. Finding a qualified successor for Lethbridge when he would be forced by RNLI statute to retire, at the age of sixty in 1984, might prove to be one of the handful of major crises that the people of the Isles of Scilly have had to face. His standards were high and his reputation was unsullied by any hint of error. Locating a man of Lethbridge's character and skills would have been hard enough in the old days; the facts of life in the late twentieth century seem to discourage the kind of independence and dedication that make such men what they are. With the appearance of huge Russian factory ships and highly efficient smaller vessels, the waters around the Scillies were becoming fished out. Meanwhile, a great influx of tourists during the 1970s had made island life expensive. Some Scillonians adjusted to the new economy and thrived, or at least made do as landlords of guest houses. Others succumbed to the temptations offered by a runaway real estate market and sold their homes to vacationers and moved to the mainland. Scillonians dependent upon fishing or flower farming for their living could but look on with amazement at the way island life had changed. They survived by performing odd jobs. At one time or another, Matt Lethbridge had been a carpenter, a boatbuilder, and a butcher besides tending his nets and traps. He and men like him had stocked the lifeboat for generations, and as they aged, fewer independent, younger men seemed to be there to replace them.

Those worries were not on Matt Lethbridge's mind when he was awakened by the telephone early on the morning of August 14. Before the honorary secretary, Tom Buckley, said anything, Lethbridge had guessed the gist of the message. He heard the wind whistling through the streets of Hugh Town, and he knew that it was about the time of the Fastnet race, whose boats he sometimes saw when he was out pulling his crayfish pots near the Bishop. Tom Buckley passed on a message from the Coastguard: a rudderless yacht named *Magic* was in distress about forty miles north-west of Round Island light.

Lethbridge pulled on his clothes. Five minutes and a fast walk later, he was in the boathouse, which stood twenty feet above the water on a point of land between Hugh Town and Porth Mellon, the old shipbuilding town. Once inside the boathouse, he walked past the tall plaques on which he, his father, and his grandfather had faithfully recorded the services of their lifeboats and past the little room with the marine radio scanner, which, like the instruments in his and every Scilly fisherman's home, automatically searched the frequencies for a transmission. Through a door was the large shed in which sat the *Guy and Claire Hunter*, high and dry on a trolley. Out of the water, she looked from below like a submarine, forty-seven feet of black and red, powerfully curving in great symmetrical rounds. There was nothing squared-off or blunt to offer unnecessary resistance to waves. A Watson-type lifeboat, she had been designed especially for this duty.

Within minutes, Lethbridge and his seven-man crew were aboard and suited up in foul-weather gear, life jackets, and safety harnesses. With him were the second coxswain, Roy Guy; the mechanic, Bill Burrow, the second mechanic, Harry Lethbridge; the bowman, Richard Lethbridge; and the crewmen, Rodney Terry and Roy Duncan. With the exception of Burrow, the mechanic, whose full-time job it was to maintain the boat, they were volunteers for the first few hours on a service, after which they would receive low pay and, if they were lucky, a reward from anybody they rescued. By tradition, they would not claim salvage on a boat even if they were entitled to it.

Down under the boat, the launchers and slipmen were preparing for the launch. They opened the boathouse doors, letting in a great blast of wind, and after warning the men on deck, let the trolly go. It slid down a ramp, out of the boathouse, and into the water. The time was 3:00 A.M. When the lifeboat drifted clear of the trolly, Matt Lethbridge, standing behind the huge steel wheel in the steering cabin, started the twin engines and pulled away from the ramp. Navigating by memory and radar, he steered through the channels between the islands, islets, and rocks of the Scillies and out into the Western Approaches.

He was not at first surprised by what he saw there. Although he could boast mildly, "Unless it's blowing about seventy, we never used to call it a gale of wind," Lethbridge had occasionally been unsettled by bad weather. A storm in 1974 left his pots hanging off a ledge on the Bishop Rock lighthouse, seventy feet above normal water level. Once he saw spume blow entirely over Trescoe Island, which is two miles long and almost a mile wide and whose maximum elevation is more than a hundred feet. The same gale blew in a four-inch-thick door in the Round Island lighthouse and lifted a hundred-pound boulder several yards up a cliff from a beach. (Later in 1979, his normally cheerful face turned grim and he became silent when he heard that two lifeboats similar to his had capsized off Scotland.) But when he spoke about the Fastnet race gale with a survivor, he said, without heroic swagger, "That was an exceptional gale for you, but it wasn't an exceptional gale for us."

Sliding at nine knots across the south-westerly seas of the predawn hours, the crew saw no boats until a small cruising yacht under storm jib came by, followed by a large sloop sailing very fast under shortened rig toward the Bishop. Lethbridge guessed that she probably was one of the leaders in the Fastnet race fleet. By 9:00 A.M., when the *Guy and Claire Hunter* was almost fifty miles north-west of Round Island, the sea was making up with a ferocity that Lethbridge had not expected. He had experienced heavier seas, waves with larger walls of breaking water, but he had not experienced so *many* breaking waves in these wind conditions. The sea, he observed, was worse than the wind strength would warrant. Several times the lifeboat's decks were awash up to her crewmen's waists, and one wave broke through the small window in the back of the helmsman's cabin, drenching and destroying Richard Lethbridge's camera, which had withstood several gales. (After the race, the second coxswain of the lifeboat based at Padstow, Cornwall, said, "extreme conditions were exceptional," in a letter about the gale to a yachting magazine.)

Lethbridge received reports from *Magic* but they were incomplete and he could not locate the rudderless yacht. His crew spotted HMS *Anglesey*, the Royal Navy fisheries protection vessel, standing by the dismasted *Bonaventure II*. When both the lifeboat and the ship were in the troughs of waves, they lost sight of the *Anglesey;* Lethbridge estimated the maximum wave height at thirty to forty feet and he overheard the *Anglesey* reporting sixty-footers.

Soon after, they located a Royal Navy helicopter hovering over a yacht named *Victride*, whose crew seemed to want to be taken off. In a dialogue over their radios, the helicopter pilot and Lethbridge agreed that the crew need not abandon the yacht, but that the lifeboat should escort her to safety. This would allow the helicopter to fly to another yacht in distress several miles away. With all the radio frequencies jammed with distress calls, Lethbridge had to concentrate hard to make out the pilot's voice and keep track of their conversation. Told that they would be escorted to port, the crew of the thirty-five-foot French yacht appeared satisfied, and they got under way under storm jib. *Victride* was knocked down several times by waves, and Lethbridge noticed that her companionway hatch was open. Since they did not have the same type of radio, there was nothing much that he could do to help. By this time, Lethbridge had become aware of the extent of the disaster; seven lifeboats had been called out. Soon after beginning to escort *Victride*, he received a radioed request for help from another yacht, *Pegasus*. Lethbridge gave *Pegasus* the course to Round Island, where all three boats made a rendezvous late on Tuesday evening, and the lifeboat led the two yachts into the harbor.

When he docked for refueling at 8:00 P.M., Lethbridge was surprised to hear that the conditions had been as bad at St. Mary's as in the Approaches. Several cruising boats had dragged their anchors and gone ashore; others had been rounded up by fishermen as they were blown across the harbor toward the beach. Brian Jenkins, a fisherman and slipway helper at the lifeboat boathouse, had even swum after a drifting yacht in order to get a tow line aboard her.

Although Lethbridge looked tired after his 17 hours of pounding, his spirits were high. With a sparkle in his eye, he told his friend Jenkins about the rough seas and how well the lifeboat had handled them. Once the fuel tanks were topped off, he was prepared to go out again immediately, and only after a

The St. Mary's lifeboat was in service for more than 19 hours on Tuesday. Twelve other lifeboats were in service for a total of more than 133 hours on Tuesday, Wednesday, and Thursday. Fatigue shows on the faces of the crew of the lifeboat on return to its station. The man holding the cup is the coxswain, Matthew Lethbridge. *Gibsons of Scilly*

brisk warning from the town's doctor did he allow his crew a
chance to change into dry clothes and eat a quick meal. By nine,
the *Guy and Claire Hunter* was back in service three miles west
of Round Island, where she made a rendezvous with *Festina
Tertia*, one of whose crew had been swept away and another,
suffering from hypothermia, taken off by a helicopter. Demoralized, cold, and exhausted, her crew requested a tow into St.
Mary's. The lifeboat crew threw a line, and soon they were un-
derway through Trescoe Channel. At one stage, the line became
tangled in the yacht's keel, and the two vessels drifted alongside
each other for a while until the snag was cleared. By midnight,
the yacht was secured at the town quay and Matt Lethbridge
and his lifeboat crew were in their homes, having been out for a
total of 19 hours, 45 minutes. The thirteen lifeboats called out
from English and Irish stations during the gale were in service
for 169 hours, 36 minutes and towed in nine yachts and escorted
nine more. Some seventy yachtsmen were aboard the yachts
towed in.

Yet an irony of the gale was that the lifeboats were not able to
perform their primary mission—to save lives. Only when trans-
ferring a few rescued sailors from commercial vessels to shore
did any lifeboats actually carry survivors; the rest of the time,
they were either searching for, escorting, or towing yachts. The
actual rescues of sailors from the water or from life rafts were
performed by helicopters, commercial vessels, or yachts. This
was true largely because the area of greatest distress was fifty to
one hundred miles from the lifeboat stations that were called
onto duty, a distance that a normal lifeboat powering at nine
knots could cover in no fewer than five or six hours but that a
helicopter could fly in less than half an hour.

A prototype of a new type of high-speed lifeboat, the fifty-
four-foot Arun, was stationed at Falmouth, on the Channel side
of Cornwall. Named the *Elizabeth Ann*, she and her crew were

---

**The crew of *Casse Tete V*, whose rudder had broken, secures the tow line from the
lifeboat *Sir Samuel Kelly*, based in Courtmacsherry, Ireland. The tow to port lasted
twelve hours.** *Ambrose Greenway*

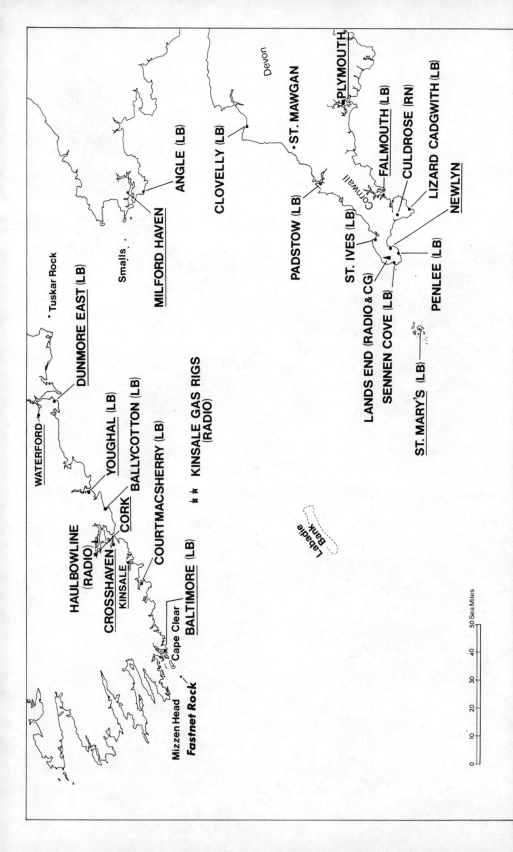

Places that feature in the search and rescue operation. Ports of refuge are underlined. "LB" indicates lifeboat stations. Land radio stations using marine radio frequencies are indicated by "Radio." St. Mawgan and Culdrose are military air bases.

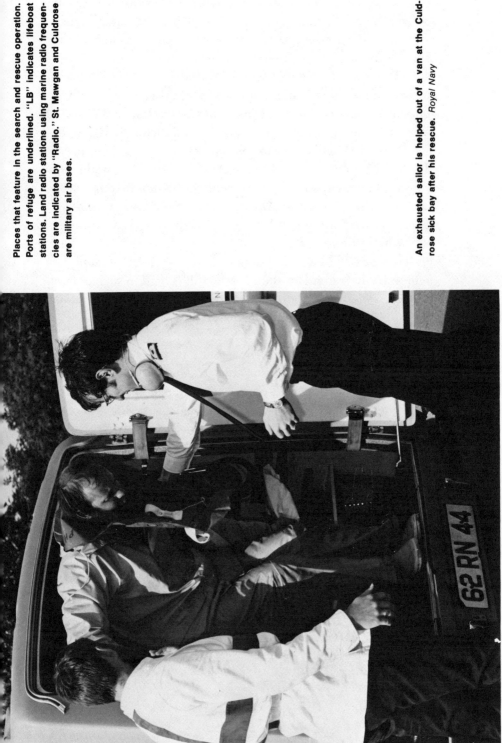

An exhausted sailor is helped out of a van at the Culdrose sick bay after his rescue. Royal Navy

offshore for more than forty-three hours during the gale, at first looking for a boy missing from a beach near Falmouth, then, after a hundred-mile sprint at seventeen knots around Land's End, searching for distressed yachts in the Western Approaches. When she towed a rudderless Swedish yacht, *Big Shadow*, into St. Mary's on Wednesday, some Scillonians were mildly offended that she and not the *Guy and Claire Hunter* performed the service, although Matt Lethbridge paid a friendly visit to the Falmouth crew and inspected their boat. Later on Wednesday, she took the abandoned *Golden Apple of the Sun* under tow from HMS *Broadsword*. On returning to Falmouth at noontime Thursday, the *Elizabeth Ann* had run four hundred and fifty miles and used a thousand gallons of fuel. Her crew had eaten only what little food they could find in the yachts. Toby West, her coxswain, told a reporter that the crew of *Big Shadow* had been warmly grateful for their rescue. "It is hard in such circumstances," West said, "to just say that you are a lifeboat doing your job." West then went back to racing a sailing fishing boat in the annual Falmouth regatta.

Perhaps if the Arun had been stationed at a more western harbor, she might have been able to get to the area of worst trouble by dawn on Tuesday, but the more maneuverable, faster helicopters would still have been the major lifesaving arm of the massive, coordinated rescue effort, which eventually involved about four thousand people and cost £350,000 ($770,000)—almost 90 percent of it expended on aircraft and the remainder expended on surface vessels.

But while seventy-four people were saved by helicopters on August 14 (one-half the number saved by Culdrose-based helicopters in all of 1978), sixty-two survivors were directly recovered by various surface vessels. These craft included eight military vessels ranging in size from Royal Navy tugs to the frigates *Overijssel* and *Broadsword*, as well as six privately owned coasters and trawlers and three yachts competing in the race. Responding to flares or Maydays, or simply chancing upon life rafts, many of the commerical vessels rescued crews and either took the survivors ashore or left them with lifeboats and re-

A search and rescue crew just off a Sea King helicopter on Tuesday. (Left to right) St. Fred Robertson, Lt. Charlie Thornton, Lt. Keith Thompson, and CPO Airman Dave Roles. These crews flew alternating missions, some staying in the air as long as four hours at a time. *Royal Navy*

sumed their course. Several naval ships stayed on station or swept designated areas during the gale. At first, the Nimrod aircraft served as on-scene commander, but on Wednesday, HMS *Broadsword*, a new Royal Navy frigate, out on sea trials, took over that role.

Communications were a major problem. At first, the Southern Rescue Co-ordination Centre at Plymouth did not have a race entry list. The list eventually provided by the Royal Ocean Racing Club showed 336 entrants, even though the club's officials believed that fewer than 310 boats had actually started the race. But which 310? Many boats that had officially withdrawn were seen sailing around the starting line; were they spectator boats or did they actually start? In any case, the start was so crowded that identification of actual racing boats was nearly impossible. To be safe, the searchers used the larger list, so they were actually looking for 33 boats that never started. Information about boats that were located was fed into a computer that had already been programmed to calculate the overall standings. During the three days of the search, the computer periodically spewed out long lists, which were distributed by automobile and helicopter to the various rescue centers at Land's End, Culdrose, and Plymouth.

Of course, these lists were only as accurate as the data fed to the computer, and much of that data was misleading. Many boats had similar names: *Golden Apple of the Sun* and *Silver Apple of the Moon; Imp* and *Impetuous;* two boats named *Pepsi* and two others named *Pinta*. Some boats had racing numbers that differed only in one number or were identical but with different nationality prefix letters. If no sail was hoisted, no number was visible. These and other problems did not make the rescuers' job any easier. Helicopter crews frequently wasted valuable time hovering over boats with indistinguishable names; airmen who dropped down to look for survivors returned to report that they had already inspected the boats. Yachtsmen's radio transmissions often were wrong or misleading, and they sometimes did not provide information about courses and speed that was necessary for lifeboats and other vessels trying to intercept them. Calculated positions were not always accurate, either. Until systematic sweeps were established on Tuesday afternoon, the search and rescue crews on and above the water were dependent upon these transmissions for locating boats in distress. So it was that in many instances luck played a more important role than any other factor in finding yachts that had requested help.

The most significant cause of the confusion was that so many boats were in distress. With 303 boats taking so much punishment in an area of about twenty thousand square miles, the huge rescue effort—said to be the largest in British waters since the evacuation of Dunkirk—was greatly taxed.

Unlike the nearly invulnerable helicopters, the ships had to endure the same seas that were damaging the yachts. HMS *Anglesey* and HMS *Broadsword* had been designed specifically for rough weather, but HNLMS *Overijssel*, the Dutch frigate on permanent guardship duty for the race, was badly strained by the storm. After being refueled by a tug on Monday evening, she steamed north-west through the fleet as the storm swept in. Her assigned task was to stay within very high frequency radio range of the Admiral's Cup boats (about forty miles in good weather), in order to take their position reports, and to radio those positions back to the mainland. There was considerable press interest in the progress of the boats in the Admiral's Cup competition, for which the Fastnet was the last and most important race.

The *Overijssel* began to roll badly as the wind and sea increased, until at one frightening moment before dawn, a wave swept over her deck and into her engine room, where the water short-circuited the generators. Rolling to within a very few degrees of the angle of heel at which she would lose all stability and capsize, she lay in the dark for twelve minutes while her engineers worked to start the generators. The return of power was a mixed blessing for those people who, like Peter Webster, the RORC's representative, stood by the radio, over which was transmitted a stream of grim news. At dawn, the Nimrod airplane flew over with its lights flashing. "Can you see a life raft?" somebody asked the Nimrod over the radio.

"We can see five life rafts," the Nimrod answered.

The *Overijssel*, a Dutch destroyer, here seen from a Royal Navy helicopter, was the Fastnet race guard ship and rescued sailors despite dangerous rolling. *A. W. Besley*

*At right, above:* A large breaker bears down on the *Overijssel* on Tuesday morning. At this time, force 10 to 12 conditions predominated, with winds gusting to over sixty knots and breaking seas that were occasionally thirty to forty feet in height. The *Overijssel* was rolling her gunwales under, and at one stage her engines shut down when the generators were flooded. *Peter Webster*

*At right, below:* A dismasted, abandoned yacht on the gray wastes of broken water. Photographs tend to diminish the apparent height of the sea, especially when taken high up (as from the *Overijssel*'s bridge) but the breaking crests as far as the eye can see give a clue about the severity of the conditions. *Peter Webster*

"It was more and more pathetic as time went by," Webster later remembered. "There were so many messages, and we could only deal with them one at a time."

Working off the scrambling nets slung over the side, the *Overijssel*'s crew recovered fifteen survivors and two bodies. The survivors were from the abandoned yachts *Trophy, Callirhoe III,* and *Polar Bear.* The last-named, like *Trophy,* was capsized as she stood by another yacht in distress. A wave picked up the stern of the thirty-three-footer and threw it over the bow. *Polar Bear* surfaced from the violent pitchpoling with her mast broken, her cabin roof ripped open by the remains of the spar, three feet of water in the cabin, and a crew member, Brigid Moreton, with a dislocated shoulder.

The injured woman's husband, *Polar Bear*'s skipper, Major John Moreton of the Queen's Dragoon Guards, decided to abandon ship. He announced the decision over marine radio, and the crew fired off a flare and inflated and boarded the life raft. They drifted without major incident for an hour until the *Overijssel* appeared and, rolling wildly, slid down to them. When her leeward side dipped, they stepped off the raft onto the scrambling nets and climbed a few feet up to the lower deck. Mrs. Moreton's arm was soon treated by a doctor picked up from another yacht.

The Dutch frigate stayed on station until the two bodies she had retrieved began to decompose badly. When she docked at Plymouth on Thursday morning, the quiet ceremony of removing the coffins from her deck gave authenticity to the disaster, about which landspeople had been hearing second- and third-hand for two days.

Among the more dreadful of those stories was that of a boat named *Bucks Fizz,* which was one of thirty-two non-Fastnet race entrants to send out distress calls heard by the coastguards. The only boat in a race for multihulls that paralleled the Fastnet race (which is open only to monohulls), *Bucks Fizz* was a thirty-eight-foot trimaran owned by Richard Pendred, who was vice-commodore of his sailing club near Rye. The light, fast three-hulled boat was seen by several Fastnet race crews during the first two days of racing, but she disappeared during the storm. At dawn on Wednesday, she was found floating upside down off the Irish coast, and two days later, an airman was dropped from a helicopter to inspect her. Nobody was aboard. Two bodies were found later and the remaining two crew members were presumed drowned. In her crew were a man and a woman who had met on the eve of the race's start in a pub in Cowes, immediately formed an attachment, and decided that it would be fun to sail together in *Bucks Fizz*.

A few crews of yachts in the race took enormous risks in responding to flares and Mayday calls from other crews. Some rescuers were themselves put in distress and had to be rescued by the military. But three crews—two English and the other one French—were brave, skillful, and fortunate enough to reach their objectives and to save a total of nineteen people from three boats, two of which sank. By coincidence, the two English boats saved French crews and the French boat saved an English crew.

At fifty-five feet in length, *Dasher* was one of the largest boats representing the military in the race. Almost every branch of the British armed forces owns yachts for leadership training or simply to allow officers to enjoy the rigors of ocean racing, and more than a dozen Fastnet race entrants represented the army, the navy, and the air force. The skipper of *Dasher*, Lieutenant Bob Hall, Royal Navy, decided to run before the seas when the weather deteriorated. At 4:30 A.M., the helmsman notified Hall that he had heard a cry for help. He shone a bright light out into the seas and soon saw a dismasted yacht approximately thirty yards away. Under storm sails, *Dasher* sailed to the yacht, which Hall identified as *Maligawa III*, a French thirty-two-footer. She was dismasted, and the glass ports in her cabin sides were smashed and her running lights were off—indications that she had suffered considerable damage. Hall shouted to the Frenchmen that he intended to take them in tow. After two practice runs in which he made sure that each crew member knew his job, Hall steered *Dasher* close alongside the French boat and a line was passed to her crew. He then headed south-east, sailing slowly under storm sails alone, with *Maligawa* comfortably in

**Helicopters and ships located and recovered several bodies of crews who had died in the water.** *A. W. Besley photographs*

tow. After forty minutes of uneventful sailing, a wave knocked *Maligawa* over on her side, throwing two of her crew overboard and flooding her with a considerable amount of water. Their shipmates hauled the two men in by their safety harness tethers. Hall decided that they were not safe, so he told the French crew to abandon ship. As their vessel started to settle deeper into the water by the stern, the six French sailors inflated their life raft, which they boarded and cut loose. The tow line was also cut, and Hall steered *Dasher* back toward the raft and, on his first try, came alongside and picked the men up without further incident. The Frenchmen were given hot drinks and dry clothes, and Lieutenant Hall assigned them to watches so they could help in sailing *Dasher,* a Camper and Nicholson 55 sloop, back to port. *Maligawa III* was later confirmed as having sunk.

At about the same time and in roughly the same part of the Western Approaches—about fifty miles southeast of Fastnet Rock—David Chatterton's *Moonstone* (like *Windswept* an Off-shore One-Design 34) was hove-to in the traditional way, with her small storm jib backed, or trimmed to windward, and the tiller lashed to leeward. She had twice been knocked down to ninety degrees. At dawn, Chatterton saw a life raft lying approximately six hundred yards to leeward. He turned on the engine, headed toward the raft, and made three attempts to get alongside, once falling off a wave with great force. Fearing a recurrence and the possibility of the boat rolling down to and over the raft, he hove-to just to windward and let a lifebuoy down to the raft on the end of a line. When the men in the raft had secured the line, *Moonstone*'s crew hauled them in. The six rescued men were from the French thirty-three-footer *Alvena*, which, they said, had been rolled over, dismasted, and, with her windows smashed in, had probably sunk. They had been in the life raft for several hours. It had capsized twice; they had righted it each time. Now loaded down with thirteen men, *Moonstone* sailed east and eventually put in at Falmouth. (*Alvena* was later recovered.)

*Griffin,* a sister ship of *Moonstone* and *Windswept,* was owned by the Royal Ocean Racing Club and commanded by an experienced Australian offshore sailor named Neil Graham, who taught sailing at Britain's National Sailing Centre, in Cowes. In his crew were two of his fellow instructors and four students from the school. All were knowledgeable, well-trained sailors. After the wind increased to force 10, they stopped racing at about 1:30 Tuesday morning. Half an hour later, Stuart Quarrie, at the helm, saw a wave whose near-vertical face was twice the height of most of the other seas. The wave fell on *Griffin*, rolling her over with such violence that the curved snap hook on the end of Quarrie's safety harness tether straightened entirely as he was thrown overboard. From five yards away, he could see *Griffin*'s keel sticking straight into the air, and her high-intensity man-overboard light blinking from under the hull in the water. Two men were trapped under the cockpit, and they soon unhooked their harnesses and swam out. The four others were inside the cabin, where, standing on the roof, they watched the water pour in the hatch. The washboards had dropped out and the hatchcover had slid forward, leaving a ten-square-foot hole that was several feet under water. After about half a minute, a wave broke against the keel and its weight slowly levered the hull upright. When she came up, the cabin was almost full of water and the deck was only three inches above the sea's level. The crew immediately decided that there was only one thing to do. The life raft was inflated, a man dove into the cabin to retrieve flares and a knife, a flare was ignited, the seven men slid into the life raft, and the bow line was cut.

About forty-five minutes later, the life raft capsized, and as they pulled it back upright, the canopy broke off and the raft changed shape from circular to tubular. They fired off one flare and, when they saw a light, several more. The light approached and became a yacht sailing under a deeply reefed mainsail.

The yacht was *Loreleï*, a thirty-six-footer owned by Alain Catherineau, from Bordeaux, one of the fifty-five French skippers who had entered the race. Built to an older and more conservative design than some of the most recent, light boats, *Loreleï* was a Sparkman and Stephens-designed She 36 built in England, and a smaller sister of *Toscana*. *Loreleï* was about forty miles south-east of the Rock at 2:00 A.M., going very fast under triple-reefed mainsail and number-4 jib through a group of boats that had stopped racing and were lying a-hull, when Catherineau spotted a flare about half a mile to leeward. He went forward with two of his crew to douse the jib, and under reefed mainsail alone they headed in the general direction of the flare, which was the first of several. Catherineau told the helmsman, Thierry Rannou, to steer about thirty degrees to one side of the flares, which appeared like a red halo over the waves, because he was not sure what type of craft had fired them off. Six hours earlier they had sailed near a fairly large French trawler; Catherineau thought that this might be the vessel in distress and, fearing collision, he did not want to get too close to her too quickly. *Lorelei* was rolling considerably, and the safety harnesses frequently offered the only support for the crew on deck. Soon the crew could make out two small lights on top of a black shape about fifty yards away: it was a life raft. They steered for the life raft and passed about ten feet to windward of it at a speed of three knots. One of the Frenchmen threw a line, but it did not reach the raft. Two of the men in the raft tried to reach the yacht, fell overboard, and were hauled back into the raft by their shipmates.

Catherineau then took the tiller because, as he later wrote in a description of the rescue, "I felt that we could recover those men, and to do that I had to take the helm of my boat and get in touch with her. I knew her well and could ask the impossible of her." He surprised Rannou by starting the engine and ordering the mainsail dropped. Rannou said that the engine could never drive *Lorelei* fast enough into the seas, and after the skipper made several futile attempts to get close to the raft, he seemed to be right. Realizing that he could not develop enough speed to steer *Lorelei* upwind, Catherineau changed tactics and instead of heading into the waves he steered parallel to them, with the wind and his unusually powerful engine pushing the sloop at five knots. About thirty yards from the raft, when he was sure that he was on the correct heading, he put the engine into reverse and the boat slowed to a stop one yard to windward of it. Two of his crew threw lines to the raft, and the men started to come aboard. Some of the men went below, but the French skipper asked the strongest of them to remain on deck to help.

The last man out of the raft was extremely weak. All he had on his upper body was a T-shirt and his safety harness, and exposure obviously had sapped his strength. He was unable even to hold his head out of the water. The French sailors hauled him on deck inch by inch every time *Loreleï* heeled (at one stage during the rescue, she was knocked down so far that the wind vane at the top of the mast was washed away). One difficulty was that, despite his hypothermia, the man refused to let go of the handholds in the life raft; his shipmates had insisted that he hold on to them, and now his hands were so tightly clenched around them that the rescuers had to pry his fingers away. They finally were able to drag him on deck and below and, to the surprise of many, he survived. It was 4:00 A.M. The Englishmen had been in the water for almost two hours, and the rescue had taken over an hour. One of the rescued sailors came on deck to thank Catherineau, shaking his hand vigorously. Exuberant at the success of their rescue mission, the French skipper and his second in command, Rannou, exchanged an emotional embrace. Not until Stuart Quarrie told the story of *Griffin's* swamping and certain foundering did Catherineau realize that he had rescued not fishermen but fellow yachtsmen.

With thirteen exhausted, wet, and in some cases seasick men on board, the French sloop was uncomfortable. The demoralized Englishmen were not the happiest of shipmates as *Loreleï* lay a-hull for much of Tuesday. When the wind started to die, Catherineau put up sail, and on Wednesday morning—some thirty hours after the rescue—she was running under spinnaker before a warm light breeze under an almost cloudless sky. Catherineau spent an hour below cleaning up the damp cabin, and then two of his crew followed him down to prepare a meal not usually served aboard racing sailboats, even by the French: *Salade de Tomates Bordelaises, Poulet Gersois, Sauté de Veau aux Carottes*, fruit, cheese, dessert, and a Médoc. Cheered by the spectacular lunch, the Englishmen finally relaxed. *Loreleï* docked at Plymouth late Wednesday night. The Englishmen found beds ashore, and the next day they borrowed money, bought wine and cigarettes, and returned to the French sloop to celebrate their rescue with Alain Catherineau and his crew.

Thanks to the courage and exemplary seamanship of other yachtsmen, the nineteen men of *Maligawa III*, *Alvena*, and *Griffin* joined the many other sailors rescued by helicopters and ships on the list of those saved during the gale. Besides *Maligawa III* and *Griffin*, three other boats sank after being abandoned. A French trawler, the *Massingy*, took seven men directly off the English yacht *Charioteer*, which went down soon after. During a capsize, *Charioteer*'s owner, Dr. J. Coldrey, had been hit on the head by the galley stove, which had come off its mountings, suffering a seven-inch cut in the scalp and a fractured cervical vertebra. *Hestrul II* sank after her six men were taken off by a helicopter. And *Magic* sank while under tow after her crew was rescued by a helicopter.

The remaining nineteen abandoned yachts were later recovered and safely towed to port by Royal Navy tugs, lifeboats, and commercial vessels. Only some of the latter claimed salvage. Claiming salvage on abandoned vessels is as legal and as encouraged now as it was a century ago, although the opportunities are fewer. Owners are happy to get their boats back, and insurance companies are always more than content to settle with the salvager for a fraction of the boat's worth rather than cover the loss of the vessel. "People think the fishermen are like vultures or scavengers," a spokesman for Lloyd's Shipping told a reporter, "but really it is an accepted procedure at sea. We would be surprised if the fishermen didn't go all out for the salvage money."

When a Cornish seaman named Bert Smidt heard that abandoned yachts were adrift in the Western Approaches, he and several crew members took his coaster, *Pirola*, out into the last of the gale. They found the abandoned *Polar Bear*, and a man went aboard the thirty-three-footer with a towline. Soon after, The *Pirola* came across the empty thirty-four-foot *Allamanda*, the procedure was repeated, and the tow headed toward Penzance. The two yachts probably were worth £60,000 ($132,000). Since he could expect the insurance companies to cover at least one-third of the cost of the boats in salvage payments, Smidt had good reason to think the trip well worth the time and risk.

But the risk increased rapidly as a second, though less violent, gale blew in on Thursday. With the two yachts tossing wildly and threatening to capsize at the end of of the towlines, Smidt ordered *Allamanda* cut loose. The man aboard rode out the storm for over ten hours before the *Pirola* returned to retrieve her as the gale died. Three days after heading out, the coaster pulled into Penzance with the two yachts. "It's an accepted part of making your living at sea," a relieved Smidt told a reporter from the *Western Morning News.* "It was dangerous, and at times I was worried about my men. I certainly didn't want to lose any of them, money or no money."

Meanwhile, a strange drama involving salvage was being played out in Milford Haven, Wales. *Camargue,* which had been abandoned by her crew as they leapt, one by one, into the water to be retrieved by a helicopter, was taken in tow on Wednesday morning by a French trawler, the *Locarec.* That afternoon, the tow pulled into the estuary of Milford Haven only to be intercepted by an English yacht, *Animal,* whose crew had relaxed after their own ordeal and now concluded that the trawler was engaged in a criminal act. The Englishmen cut the towline, put their own line aboard the yacht, and *Camargue* up the estuary. The French claimed salvage, and the local Receiver of Wrecks, a government official, reclaimed *Camargue,* and the Department of Trade, which has jurisdiction over salvage, said that the act of piracy in reverse was unprecedented and that it did not know what course of action to follow. As was the case with most of the rescues conducted during the Fastnet gale, the story had a satisfactory ending: the French fishermen received some compensation for their time and efforts and the owner retrieved his boat.

# 8 ARIADNE: The Unluckiest Boat in the World

ONE BOAT, *Ariadne,* benefited little from the huge, heroic rescue effort, but like everything else that affected the thirty-five-foot American yacht, what happened was nobody's fault. *Ariadne* was owned by a sixty-one-year-old American named Frank Ferris (nicknamed "Hal") who lived in London. An enthusiastic sailor who had raced extensively in the United States, Ferris had saild *Ariadne* and an earlier boat out of West Mersea, in Essex, for several racing seasons. Not tied to his home waters, he had raced his boats in the Solent, on the North Sea, and in Scandinavia. Doing moderately well and carrying the distinctive "US" nationality prefix letters on her sails and a New York hailing port on her transom, *Ariadne* was known in British sailing circles as "that Yank boat from Mersea." She had been built of laminated plywood in Scotland and had been designed by an American named Dick Carter, whose greatest successes had been in Britain. By the standards of the late 1970s, *Ariadne* was a beautiful boat, with traditional varnished topsides on which her name was written in large white script letters. In the fleets of chalky-white fiberglass and brightly colored aluminum boats, she was a stunning example of classic appearance melded into modern shapes and materials.

Hal Ferris was serious about his racing; that was obvious to any sailor who studied *Ariadne,* even in her near-wrecked state after the Fastnet race as she lay against a dirty wharf in Penzance. Ferris had given her the most secure hatches to keep the ocean out, the best winches, blocks, and hydraulic equipment with which to trim and shape sails, and the most sophisticated instruments with which to measure boat performance and wind

---

PRECEDING PHOTOGRAPH: *Ariadne* racing earlier in the 1979 season. *Eric North*

speed and direction. Much of that gear had been installed during the previous winter by Ferris and his crew, which consisted
of friends and business associates, most of whom were experienced sailors.

All were Englishmen except for Ferris and Robert Robie,
a sixty-three-year-old American oil company executive. Bob
Robie had learned to sail at Vineyard Haven, Massachusetts, on
the island of Martha's Vineyard, and he came from a sailing family. His brother, Ted, was a member of the Vineyard Haven
Yacht Club crew that won the North American Junior Sailing
Championship in 1933 and 1934, and another brother, Bud,
carried on the tradition by serving in the winning crews in 1935
and 1936. (By coincidence, the skipper of the second-place crew
in 1935 was my father. By further coincidence, I crewed for Bob
Robie's former sailing instructor, Bill Cox, in the winning boat
in the 1974 North American Match-Racing Championship.) Bud
Robie was killed in World War II, and Ted Robie moved inland,
but Bob Robie never lost his enthusiasm for sailing. He owned
or chartered cruising boats in Cuba, the Canary Islands, and
wherever else he could during a long, peripatetic career in the
oil industry. When the Iranians nationalized their oil fields after
the 1979 revolution, Robie lost his job, but he was satisfied that
he now had more time available to help his friend Hal Ferris
prepare *Ariadne* for the 1979 racing schedule, the high point of
which would be the Fastnet race. He was retiring soon anyway,
and planned to move with his wife of thirty-six years to the
resort island of Hilton Head, South Carolina, on the southeast
coast of the United States, where he hoped to start a sailing
school. A friend of Robie's, Kingman Brewster, the United
States ambassador to Great Britain and a former president of
Yale University, had been asked to sail in *Ariadne*, but was unable to join Ferris's crew due to an unexpected meeting in
Washington.

The youngest crew member invited aboard *Ariadne* was
nineteen-year-old Matthew Hunt, a gentle, mature young man
who had sailed dinghies at West Mersea. The son of a doctor and
a nurse, and the brother of another nurse, Matthew was himself

applying to medical school. Flattered by Ferris's invitation and
excited by the prospect of sailing in a Fastnet race, he also had
the time available to sail in *Ariadne* throughout most of her am-
bitious racing schedule.

The Royal Ocean Racing Club exists primarily to run ocean
races, the most important of which and the cause of the club's
founding is the Fastnet. A boat that sails in all the club's races
and in other races sponsored by English and French yacht
clubs will be busy almost every weekend from May through September. In a Fastnet race year, a well-organized skipper will use
the early-season races to test his boat and crew for the Fastnet.
That is what Hal Ferris did in 1979. *Ariadne* competed in the
North Sea, Cowes-Dinard, and Channel races, as well as in a
week of competition among the Channel Islands that was sponsored by a French organization. Most of *Ariadne*'s Fastnet crew
were aboard for one or more of the early races, and Matthew
Hunt sailed in many. But the entire crew of six had never been
together before they assembled for the Fastnet start on August
11. In common they held a liking for the rigors of ocean racing,
and affection for Hal Ferris, who was a good skipper in a sport
that is, unfortunately, full of martinets. Cheerful and willing to
delegate responsibility and listen to advice, he was decisive in
situations that called for strong leadership. All in all, Ferris was
the captain of a happy vessel. Ferris and Robie, the two Americans, were the oldest members of the crew. Two had come long
distances to race. Twenty-three-year-old Rob Gilders, who had
sailed in Ferris's boats for seven years, flew to England from the
island of St. Martin's, in the Caribbean, where he was a sailmaker, and David Crisp arrived from Vienna, Austria. The sixth
crew member was forty-three-year-old Bill Le Fevre. Despite
considerable sailing experience, most of them had not sailed in a
Fastnet race. In the case of Bob Robie, sailing a Fastnet was a
goal that, as he approached old age and was preparing to move
back to the United States, he might never again be able to attain.

The six men were divided into two two-man watches, with
the skipper and the navigator, David Crisp, serving as "floaters"

to help out on deck when necessary. During the easy first two days of the race, the crew ate well, rested, and kept a happy bantering as the thirty-five-foot sloop beat into the light wind, down the Devon and Cornish coasts. Few boats were in sight until the wind died to a flat calm Monday morning, when the crew was satisfied to see many larger competitors drifting nearby.

When the wind came up around noon on Monday, they set the reaching jib and were able to sail the course for Fastnet Rock at *Ariadne*'s maximum speed. The air chilled and water started to come on deck, so the crew bundled up in their foul-weather gear and safety harnesses. Bob Robie, in fact, always wore his safety harness under his foul-weather jacket, anticipating that he would have to hook onto the boat any time that the sea was rough enough to throw spray on deck.

With the wind directly over the beam pushing *Ariadne* over, around, and sometimes under the long swells rolling in from the Atlantic Ocean, they had a fast, exciting ride Monday afternoon and evening. Bill LeFevre suffered from some seasickness, but not, his shipmates were happy to see, as badly as he had in the Channel race, a week before the Fastnet start. Ferris had given LeFevre a new batch of pills that appeared to be doing their job well.

At around 10:00 P.M., the wind increased dramatically, and the crew tied a reef in the mainsail and dropped the reaching jib, putting up in its place the relatively small number-3 jib. But even that was too much, and they soon decreased the area of the number 3 by reefing the sail and started to work reefing the mainsail further. But the mainsail split. Flogging madly in two parts in the by now force 8 wind, the main was useless, and all hands were called on deck to claw the sail down. This was discouraging. The boat required the mainsail to keep racing in those conditions, which, though rough and difficult, were not bad enough to cause real concern. It was too rough, however, for Rob Gilders, the sailmaker, to start stitching the sail back together.

They carried on under the reefed number-3 jib for an hour,

the conditions deteriorating rapidly until *Ariadne* could not be held on her course to Fastnet Rock. Just after midnight, David Crisp heard the BBC shipping bulletin. He stuck his head through the companionway and said, "Bad news. Force 8 and 9, locally force 10." The pointer was frequently touching sixty on *Ariadne*'s anemometer.

Almost immediately Hal Ferris said, "Let's pack it in." There was no objection. *Ariadne* was run off directly before the wind, the number-3 was doused and the number-4 jib was set in its place. But as the wind continued to increase, with the anemometer now registering a steady sixty—its dial could read no higher—Matthew Hunt and David Crisp soon hoisted the tiny storm jib. This was a long, exhausting sail change. They pulled down the number-4 jib, dragged it aft, and shoved it down the main hatch. Opening the forward hatch would have allowed too much water below. While the storm jib was being rigged, *Ariadne*, under bare poles, moved through the waves more comfortably. But Hal Ferris feared that they were closing too quickly on the Irish coast and, remembering the seamen's rule that a vessel is always safer offshore than near land, he wanted the storm jib up so he could steer away from shore. When daylight came in five or six hours, they could decide which harbor to head for. Perhaps it would be Crosshaven, which Matthew Hunt knew well. His father had been born there and Matthew visited Crosshaven frequently.

The greatest danger they faced was not from the wind or the waves but rather from the other boats around them. Running off before the wind with not much control over *Ariadne*'s heading, they came across other yachts under even less control. The red and green running lights would appear and disappear behind waves with maddening irregularity, and shouting accomplished nothing in the screech of the gale and the roar of the waves. There were several close calls.

For several hours, Hal Ferris's tactic of running before it was successful. At 2:00 A.M., the storm jib ripped right down its luff. Matthew Hunt, resting below (the boat's motion was comfortable enough to permit sleep), was awakened by the clatter of the torn sail and rushed on deck to haul it down. To slow *Ariadne*, they tied the sail to lines and dragged it over the stern. Hunt returned below to doze off in his foul-weather gear.

Sometime later, he awoke in a chaos of flying objects, his world turned upside down. *Ariadne* had been caught under the curl of a rogue wave and rolled over. On deck, Rob Gilders, hit by the wave just as he stood to light a cigarette, was thrown overboard to the limit of the tether of his safety harness and David Crisp, at the tiller, was trapped under the boat. Crisp was just at the end of the long breath he had taken when *Ariadne* righted herself. Gilders pulled himself aboard, and the remainder of the crew, below, tried to take stock of the situation.

The only man injured was LeFevre, but that was serious. A head wound left him bleeding and badly stunned on the cabin sole. Hunt, the doctor's son, thought that the wound perhaps was fatal. They all immediately saw they were in trouble. Water was up to their waists. It had come in through the ventilators and the large opening left by the smashed washboards.

Hunt and Gilders quickly began to clean out the cabin, throwing soggy sleeping bags, clothes, and other items into the cockpit for the others to heave overboard. As the badly injured LeFevre, already weakened by seasickness, searched for flares and life jackets that had been thrown out of their lockers by the force of the capsize, Hunt and Gilders bailed out the cabin with a bucket and a sauce pan. When the water level dropped to below the pump handle, they pumped, too. In the cockpit, Robie and Ferris tried to clean up the rigging and to cheer up the others. The mast had broken in two places, and the middle section had gone overboard leaving relatively little mess on deck.

After an hour or so, at 5:30 A.M., the sky began to lighten, and with the water level gradually dropping in the cabin, spirits improved. The life jackets and flares were found in remote corners of the cabin and were issued to all hands. Somebody laughed and said that all Englishmen should be thankful for gales since a storm off the Irish coast had defeated the Spanish Armada in 1588.

Suddenly, *Ariadne* was rolled over again through a quick 360-degree spin. David Crisp and Bob Robie, sitting in the cockpit, were flipped over the lifelines into the sea. Crisp was towed along by the tether of his safety harness; when *Ariadne* righted herself, he was dragged aboard by his crewmates. But Bob Robie, the man who would not go on deck without wearing his harness, was lost. Perhaps his tether broke, or the object to which he had been secured pulled out, but whatever the cause his previously trustworthy safety system failed. When *Ariadne* righted herself, those on deck frantically searched for him. Robie soon appeared fifty yards away on the crest of a wave. He waved, they waved back, he dropped into the trough, and he was never seen again.

Dazed by a blow to his head, Matthew Hunt stumbled on deck. He came to alertness with somebody shouting into his face, "This is the Fastnet race! *This is the Fastnet race!!*"

Dejected and exhausted, Hal Ferris sat in the cockpit, his endurance limited by his age and the effects of an automobile accident that had occurred several years earlier. In the worst storm of his long sailing career, as he described it to his crew, his boat twice had been rolled over. The first time, she had lost her rig had been half filled with water. The second time, he had lost a friend and shipmate.

By 6:00, in the increasing light, they could see huge, frothing seas like those that had shattered *Ariadne* in the darkness of the night. The mast and rigging lay in pieces on deck and, below, the cabin was in shambles and, despite their bailing, had water up to the settee berths. One crew member was badly injured and the other four were shivering and enervated. It was a time to wonder how much more they, he, and *Ariadne* could take of this storm.

Hal Ferris made his decision. He told the crew that it was time to abandon ship. Nobody disagreed.

The life raft was pulled out from under the mainsheet traveler in the cockpit and the inflation line was pulled. The rubber raft inflated perfectly and was dropped over the side. The five men gingerly climbed in, the bow line was cut, and the raft and

**Ariadne adrift after her abandonment.** *A. W. Besley*

the hulk that was once the beautiful *Ariadne* drifted away from each other.

Morale improved immediately. The raft's motion was much more comfortable than *Ariadne*'s, and the partial shelter provided by the tentlike canopy was a comfort after the exposed cockpit. From time to time, a wave splashed water into the raft and the crew bailed it and Bill LeFevre's blood out with a small bucket they had found in an emergency kit, which also held flares and food. LeFevre was obviously in pain, and the others did what they could to comfort him with forecasts of rescue.

About two hours after abandoning *Ariadne*, Rob Gilders was bailing out the raft when, with his head outside the canopy, he saw a small freighter a few hundred yards away. "I see a coaster," he shouted to the men inside the canopy. He was handed a red flare, which he lit. The German coaster, named *Nanna*, headed in the direction of the raft.

Just then, the life raft capsized. Whether because it was hit by an especially bad wave or because the men in their excitement suddenly shifted position, the raft turned upside down. Gilders, the only man who was not hooked to the raft by his safety harness, was thrown several feet away but he swam back and climbed onto the bottom of the raft. David Crisp ended up under the raft, his head safely in the air bubble. The three others were hooked to the raft, pulled themselves back, and held on to the handholds lashed to the inflated rings.

All five men stayed where they were to conserve their strength for the difficult job ahead: a lunge to *Nanna*'s ladder and a long climb up to safety.

The captain of the coaster skillfully brought the *Nanna* right alongside the raft, moving ahead slowly to maintain steerage way. Rob Gilders leapt onto the ladder from the bottom of the overturned raft, just catching the rungs. He laboriously pulled himself up the heaving, rolling topsides of the coaster and into the arms of her crew.

Ferris was the next to try to escape from the sea. He unhooked his safety harness from the life raft and lunged, half swimming, for the bottom rungs of the ladder, but he failed. Either missing the rungs or smashed by the rolling coaster, or both, Hal Ferris was swept away. His crew last saw him fifty yards away.

The coaster swept by and swung around in a great arc to make another pass at the raft. Matthew Hunt pulled himself up on the bottom, but when the *Nanna* came by, she rolled away from the raft and her ladder was high over his head. All he could do was fend off the coaster's topsides and bottom with his feet, to keep the raft from being pulled into her propellers.

As the coaster swung around for her third rescue attempt, Hunt pulled Bill LeFevre out of the water and onto the bottom. LeFevre seemed alert, and he helped Hunt haul the greatly weakened David Crisp, who had come out from under the raft, up on the rubber platform. Hunt told them both to hook their safety harnesses to a strap glued to the bottom of the raft so that they would not be swept away if they were washed off.

Lying on his side, watching the *Nanna* slowly curve to him, young Matthew Hunt knew this was his last chance for survival. He felt numb all over, and the desire to lay back and go to sleep was almost overpowering. He saw the coaster turn toward him, first her plunging bow, and then her rolling topsides, and then the ladder, at the top of which, on deck, stood men beckoning and yelling, "Jump! *Jump! This is the last chance! You must jump!"*

Hunt unhooked his safety harness from the strap and turned to Crisp and LeFevre and told them to be sure to do the same before they left the raft. As the coaster's ladder slipped by, Hunt jumped for a high rung while Crisp leapt for a lower rung.

Hunt slowly crawled up the ladder and into the hands of *Nanna*'s crew. Finally secure, he looked down and, to his horror, saw that David Crisp, halfway up the ladder, was still attached to the life raft by the tether of his safety harness. The life raft jerked away from the ship, the tether tightened and pulled Crisp down into the water, and he, Bill LeFevre, and the raft were swept under the ship's stern.

For the first time since the storm hit *Ariadne,* Matthew Hunt felt helpless. Suddenly cold after hours of numbness, he

staggered below with Rob Gilders, wrapped in blankets provided by the *Nanna*'s crew. They were given hot drinks and
food, and a crewman vacated his cabin for them. They slept for
hours. When they were awakened late Tuesday night, the 180-
foot German coaster was steaming up the English Channel. The
gale had died. The *Nanna*'s international crew of Africans and
Europeans, who communicated in Pidgin English, told them
that they would be dropped off on a lifeboat that would take
them to the mainland. Hunt and Gilders, the only survivors of
*Ariadne*, were picked up by the Lizard lifeboat at 1:00 A.M. on
Wednesday, a bit more then twenty-four hours after Hal Ferris
had decided to abandon the race. They were taken ashore, given
money, and put on trains for home.

# 9 The Finishers: Retreat and Refuge

**A**T EIGHT TUESDAY MORNING, in *Toscana*, Eric Swenson's watch had finished breakfast and were pulling off layers of wet clothing in eager anticipation of a long sleep, when they heard a news program broadcast over the Irish radio service. Three men were dead in the Fastnet race, the announcer said, and many more were missing. Swenson switched on the marine radio to an emergency frequency in time to hear a flat, matter-of-fact voice say, "We have taken two on board. Two others went under my stern."

John Coote, the navigator, slid open the hatch, stuck his head out, and told my watch, "Men are dying out here."

Standing behind the steering wheel in our force 10 world, I could make no sense of this report. So engaged were we in our own struggles with sea and wind that even believing that other boats were also out in the gale was difficult. Anyway, I told myself, this storm was not so bad. I measured it against the four gales I had previously experienced: one in the Gulf of Tehuantepec, off Mexico, in February 1964; another near Bermuda later that same year; a storm during the 1972 Bermuda Race; and the force 9 blow during the Cowes Week race five days earlier. No doubt about it, this was the worst one, but if we were surviving others should survive. There must have been a freak accident.

The barometer had been rising since 4:30, our logbook recorded, at a rate of almost 3 millibars (0.1 of an inch) an hour, just as rapid as the precipitous drop between 5:00 P.M. Monday and 3:00 A.M. Tuesday. The storm center had passed, yet the wind was still in the mid-fifties as *Toscana* ran down mountainous seas, frothing, boiling, snapping at her stern. The cold

---

PRECEDING PHOTOGRAPH: **Waves breaking near *Casse Tete V* on Tuesday morning.**
*Ambrose Greenway*

wind blew spray off the breakers and our wake and onto my back, where the droplets stung like BBs through the layers of damp clothes. With most of the waves from astern and lengthening out, steering was easier than it had been the previous night, and in daylight the helmsman could now see them and look for smooth paths to run along. We took turns steering, changing every hour or so, and we were warmed and thrilled by our mad surges down the Matterhorns, over the Rockies, and around the Everests. The bow wave thundered.

The sky cleared in midmorning. The blue-green water and white breakers reflected the sun's rays with the blinding dazzle of a snow-covered mountaintop. At about eleven, a gigantic rainbow appeared astern, arching across the horizon. Never before had I seen a full rainbow—they always seem to begin or end somewhere out of sight—and I took this one, straddling our wake like the Colossus of Rhodes, to be a protective sign.

By then the radio had reported half a dozen deaths and several sinkings, and we saw with our own eyes that other boats were vulnerable. *Marionette, Silver Apple of the Moon,* and several yachts whose hulls were hidden by waves lay under bare poles on either side of our heading as we swept along at ten knots. Some seemed to be abandoned; others had one or two men in the cockpit and were riding it out. We tried to raise them on the radio, but there was no answer. Soon after, we discovered that the antenna of our very high frequency radio (the only kind that most British yachts carry) had been blown off the mast. Eric reported their and our positions to the Land's End Coastguard station over the medium frequency radio that *Toscana* carried to meet the requirements of American ocean races.

Because the wind seemed to lighten a bit—and also because we were getting used to it after some twelve hours of force 11 to 12 gusts—we gradually increased sail area by shaking out reefs. John Ruch and I tried to set the number-4 jib, but it ripped where it fed into the slot on the headstay and we carried on under forestaysail. By 4:00 P.M. the wind clearly was easing as the gale swept away from us, and we were left with that half-empty feeling that comes at the end of any great experience, good or bad. At 7:00 P.M., when my watch came on deck after a restful six hours below, *Toscana* was averaging about eight knots in a force 7 wind. Astern were a handful of unidentifiable boats, and to leeward was Edward Heath's *Morning Cloud*, unmistakable with her sail numbers clear to the naked eye. While we sailed a bit above the course to keep the forestaysail full, she ran dead before the wind with her jib hanging uselessly from the headstay. Her crew, we decided, was not trying very hard; perhaps a report we had heard about a damaged rudder was true and they were nursing her home at low speed.

With about thirty-five knots of wind and easy steering, we began to discuss the possibility of setting the spinnaker. Eric agreed, and with the entire crew on deck we set a heavyweight large spinnaker without problem. When the boats astern saw that it could be done, they too hauled up their spinnakers. Each sail was of a distinctive color. The boat three miles astern, with a blue and gold spinnaker, was *Alliance,* a fifty-four-footer sailed by midshipmen and officers from the United States Naval Academy.

We were surprised that the crew of *Morning Cloud* made no motion toward setting more sail. Perhaps she was being steered with emergency equipment and was heading inside the Scillies for Penzance, Falmouth, or some other close port. With our speed increased by a knot or so by the spinnaker, we gradually pulled away from her. Just at sunset, we spotted the white light revolving around the top of the Bishop's Rock lighthouse about ten miles off our port bow, and a bit later we jibed onto port tack to cut around the Isles of Scilly.

The wind continued to fade, but the seas remained high for hours and rolled the by now slow-moving *Toscana* uncomfortably so that we could not sail dead downwind without having the force 3 breeze shaken out of the sails. After my watch came on for the dawn watch at 3:00 A.M. Wednesday, we exerted ourselves for a couple of hours trying to find the heading for the greatest speed. When we and *Toscana* finally settled down, we slipped east at six knots on an easy beam reach, and waited for the dawn.

It was an estuary rather than ocean dawn—warm air breathing lightly over almost flat water, land in sight to leeward, the unresisting wheel held with one hand while the other raised a coffee mug to the helmsman's lips. John Ruch awakened John Coote, who decided that he would give Francie the morning off and make breakfast. Sitting quietly in the cockpit and on deck, we smelled hash and eggs through the open hatches and squinted in the unfamiliar sunlight at the competitors nearby, trying to identify them and guess how we were doing. At 6:15, Susan awakened Eric's watch. They came on deck forty-five minutes later, spouting compliments for Coote's breakfast and looking around our horizon with the cheery curiosity of the well rested and fed. My watch put on a little show for them by changing from the heavy to the light spinnaker—normally a five-man job—with only our four people. At one stage during the operation, I secured one line with my teeth and held two other lines and the steering wheel in my hands. The performance earned laughter and applause, although (of course) some spoilsport had to describe how he had once changed spinnakers with only three people. Then Eric slipped in beside me at the wheel and I told John, Susan, and Nick that we could go below and sample Coote's culinary delights and kid him about his angel food birthday cake, which he had sat on during the gale. Over breakfast, Nick talked about the pleasures of golf, and I said that I didn't play golf but had always wanted to learn dry-fly fishing. We ate the eggs and hash, and complimented Coote, and went to our bunks. I threw my clothes in a soggy heap, toweled myself off, and pulled on my nightshirt. The forward toilet was broken and the after one was leaking, so I went on deck to relieve myself. Eric took one look at me in my Scotch-plaid nightshirt and said, "What is this apparition? Something from the *Arabian Nights*?" Everybody laughed, and I responded, "Somebody's got to add a little culture around here." They all laughed again, and leaving them on the level deck in the warm sun, I went below, crawled into my bunk, and went right to sleep.

All in all, it was the best kind of ocean-racing morning: fine weather, comfortable sailing, excellent food, good shipmates;

and not once did anybody mention what we had all known since Tuesday evening: that fifteen people had died, twenty-four boats had been abandoned, and hundreds of crews were unaccounted for somewhere behind us in the Western Approaches. It was our dirty little secret, and by silent agreement we were not going to discuss it until we reached shore.

At 3:24 that warm afternoon, when *Toscana* finished at Plymouth's breakwater after a lovely day's sail, it was almost like the end of any other race. We quietly coiled the sheets and folded the sails as Eric switched on the engine and steered *Toscana* into the end of a long raft-up of boats tied to each other, side to side. We pulled in next to a Dutch yacht, and exchanged the usual pleasantries as they took our lines: "When did you finish? How did you do? Where were you when . . . ?" Eric pulled a bottle of rum out of the liquor locker, and Francie, in her bikini, brought mugs and glasses into the cockpit, and everybody but myself settled down to the postrace drink. "Eric," I said, "I think I should get ashore." He said, "All right. See you later." I clambered over the lifelines to the Dutch boat and across the decks of the other ten boats to a slippery ladder that ran up the bulkhead.

When I reached the wharf, all semblance between this and any other race immediately ended. Solitary women stood nervously shifting their weight from one foot to the other, looking out toward the Channel. Small groups of people huddled in somber conferences. Men holding notebooks or television cameras stopped other men in sailing clothes and asked questions. A tall man with a notebook asked me if I had been in the race. I said that I had. He opened the notebook and identified himself as a reporter from the *Los Angeles Times;* could he ask me some questions? I told him that I was on my way to the press room to telephone a report to the *New York Times,* but I was sure they would not mind if I talked to him. He asked me to describe the winds and seas, and I did. Did we have any trouble? None. What did I know about the deaths? Nothing.

And I didn't, and for a long while neither did anybody else, but when I found the press room in the Duke of Cornwall Hotel and read some of the newspapers that were scattered about, I could see that the American reporter's approach to the race was especially cautious. Bitterly competing for circulation, the London-based, English national newspapers were out in force. Among the headlines were: "Fastnet Race of Death: 30 lives feared lost . . . 21 boats missing as a near hurricane hits yachtsmen"; "9 Die in Yacht Race Havoc: Boats sunk and abandoned as 80 mph gale lashes Western Approaches"; "The Suicide Armada"; "Victim of the Cruel Sea"; "Sinking of the Armada"; and "Cauldron of Death." For the first two days, many reporters covered the storm and its havoc as they would have approached any mishap in some remote or vaguely understood place—a mine disaster, say, or an accident in a nuclear power plant. They hovered around the gateway, buttonholing survivors and experts in an attempt to find out what had happened. Survivors at Culdrose, in Ireland, or in Milford Haven told grim stories that made gripping reading. Yet under pressure to explain how such a calamity could possibly happen, the reporters—few of whom understood weather or boats—were necessarily dependent upon yachtsmen who had not sailed in the race and whose opinions may not have had much to do with reality.

One of these sources was John Maltby, sales director of the Beaufort Air Sea Equipment Company, a manufacturer of life rafts (including ours in *Toscana*). He was quoted in the August 16 *Guardian* as saying, "No yachtsman in his right mind should go out in that sort of weather, because no survival equipment can make up for human exhaustion." Maltby went on to chide the Royal Ocean Racing Club for not calling off the race when a force 7 gale was forecast. People could not take that kind of punishment. "From the empty rafts being brought in," he said, referring to life rafts, "there would seem to be backing for my belief that the equipment was stronger than the human beings." Maltby could not possibly have known at the time he gave this interview that his company had made a life raft that had broken up—the raft under *Trophy*'s crew, two of whom were swept away to their deaths and one of whom died of exposure.

A broader perspective was offered by Des Sleightholme, the

editor of the British yachting magazine *Yachting Monthly*, who told a *Guardian* reporter that this was an exceptional storm that hit at the wrong time: "Let's face it. If there was not a race going through that area at that time, most people would never have known the storm was taking place." Although some sailors appeared to agree with Sleightholme—Jim Hardy, a crew member on the Australian Admiral's Cup team, quoted Lord Byron: "Man marks the earth with ruin; his control stops at the shore"—a few survivors came ashore with strong opinions that somebody was at fault. The consensus seemed to be that modern racing boats were unseaworthy or dangerous and that competition drove many Fastnet sailors to take unnecessary risks. Tom McLoughlin, a young sailor from California who had been a helmsman in the French boat *Accanito*, was quoted in the *Daily Mail* and *Daily Mirror* on August 16: "We were warned three days ago that there would be force 8 gales, and yet many of us deluded ourselves into thinking that the weather was going to improve. Some continued racing after it became clear that it was pointless to do so. Many small boats put to sea and sailed into conditions they knew to be dangerous. The people I respect are the ones who quite the race. The competitive urge can be a very unbalancing thing, and we are all guilty in a way of not respecting the sea enough."

This self-rebuke—*Accanito* lost her rudder and was sailed and towed into Crosshaven—was temperate compared with the criticisms that some survivors hurled at other Fastnet crews and their boats, presumably the ones that suffered fatalities. Said one survivor, "Some of the Fastnet participants put to sea in clothes baskets. The rigging, steering, and strength of their boats were not up to the job." Another opinion: "One of the reasons for such loss of life and damaged boats is that a certain amount of safety is being sacrificed in the search for speed. There is a tremendous quest for more and more speed and so boats are being built much lighter. But materials are being used that have not been proved in the twisting contortions of a yacht in an ocean storm." (The unproven material referred to is carbon fiber, a strong lightweight substance that had been used in the

construction of rudders; almost half of the fourteen broken rudders in the race were made of this material. Little other major
damage had been reported.)

"Too Much Emphasis on Speed" was the headline over John
Ahern's yachting column in the August 19 *Boston Sunday
Globe*. Ahern quoted Ted Hood, an American yacht designer
and sailmaker who did not sail in the Fastnet race: "More and
more I've noticed that racing yachts are being designed for
speed rather than strength, and the game has been building
toward a disaster such as the Fastnet for quite a while." Hood
also told Ahern that ocean-racing crews are not properly prepared for emergencies. "He is correct," Ahern amened.

In the same column, Ted Turner was given space to expound
on the same theme. His *Tenacious* stood up all right, he said.
"It's those dishonest little things, skinned-out hulls to save
weight, that can't take it. There's got to be some legislation
against them. And there has to be something done about the
people who go to sea and haven't had the experience. Designers
have to change the emphasis from speed to safety. This tragedy
will bring about changes. But this situation should never have
been allowed to exist."

Turner had been speaking to reporters on that theme almost
from the moment *Tenacious* docked at Plymouth after finishing
the race at 10:30 Tuesday night. Colorful, articulate, and opin-
ionated, he was a celebrity among both sailors and the general
public and always made good copy. Turner had been a cham-
pion ocean-racing sailor since he entered the sport in the mid-
1960s and was the winning helmsman in the 1977 America's
Cup. At the age of forty-one, he had amassed a small fortune and
a large following through his ownership of a successful television
station, whose programs were beamed across the United States
by satellite, and of two professional athletic teams in his home
city of Atlanta, Georgia. A self-proclaimed defender of traditional values and gentlemanly virtues, Turner had in 1977
openly questioned the honesty of Lowell North, a sailmaker and
an opposing skipper in the America's Cup eliminations, after
North had been forced by his own boat's managers to refuse

personally to make sails for Turner's boat, *Courageous.* Speaking as skipper of his own highly successful, seven-year-old *Tenacious*, Turner had often criticized competitors who, he thought, cut corners solely to win races.

For a while after he finished, Turner's main concern was whether or not *Tenacious* had won the Fastnet Race on corrected time. When a much smaller boat was mistakenly listed as winning, he prepared to fly back to the United States. Turner cheered up and decided to stay in Plymouth after the Royal Ocean Racing Club discovered the error. Later, when a *New York Times* reporter asked him what had been his worst moment in the race, Turner responded, "When I was told that some little boat was the winner. I had four hours of bitter disappointment before it was straightened out. It was a big sea all right," he went on, "but we pressed on and never thought about stopping racing. One or two were seasick, but at the height of the storm we had a steak dinner."

Turner told United Press International, "Like any experience, whenever you come through it you feel better. We're not talking about the other people who died, but to be able to face it all and come through it is exhilarating. Sailing in rough weather is what the sport is all about."

On Friday, Turner was interviewed via satellite on the American Broadcasting Company television show *Good Morning, America.* The host, David Hartmann, asked him if he had been afraid during the race.

"We made it okay," Turner responded.

Hartmann repeated the question.

"I guess I'm more afraid of being afraid than actually being afraid," Turner answered vaguely. "But I was concerned. I wasn't too concerned about our survival, because they said that the worst it would be is force 10, and the waves are the biggest problem. You never know exactly what shape they're going to take. We got hit by quite a few that knocked our boat literally flat."

Despite his admission that *Tenacious* had not always been under complete control, Turner continued to sound the theme

**Ted Turner.** *Louis Kruk*

that the gale had not threatened him. "You always feel bad when your fellow yachtsmen drown. But you never can really be completely prepared for what nature has in store. We knew it was coming. We listened to weather forecasts. But four people died on land, and how can you prepare for something like that—trees falling and walls falling?"

"It was rough, r-u-f-f," he said in another interview. "It wasn't a pleasure cruise, but we had a good crew and a good, big boat. I always wanted a big boat. From what I can tell, it seems the smaller boats were the ones that got into trouble here."

In an article that he signed in the October issue of *Motor Boating & Sailing*, an American yachting magazine, Turner wrote, "I remember saying to the crew that twenty men would die that night. Regretfully, those turned out to be prophetic words." Despite being knocked flat six or seven times, he wrote, his primary fear was that of running down smaller boats in the night. "If we hit one of those lightly constructed fiberglass boats, *Tenacious* would crush it, smash it in two and everybody aboard would be killed. Of all the things that happened that night, that was my greatest fear, and that is the only thing that had me scared—that, and the fear that something aboard *Tenacious* might break, causing us to lose the race."

Turner concluded the article with a bit of self-congratulation: "You're supposed to have a strong vessel with crew and equipment for any condition. I feel a little like Noah. I knew that the flood was coming, and I had a boat ready that would get me through it.

"It was a storm precisely like this one that saved England from the Spanish Armada. Whenever you sail in the English Channel, you've got to be prepared for the return of that storm."

At any other time, Ted Turner's glorying in his boat, his first-place trophy, and himself might have been interpreted as a successful athlete's boyish pride, but in the context of the Fastnet race tragedies it was widely viewed as insensitive and callous. There is, however, another perspective, as Pete Axthelm, the sports columnist for the American magazine *Newsweek*, pointed out. Axthelm was shocked at first when he read the following quote by Turner: "This is the greatest sailing accomplishment in a long time. We weren't really concerned with the conditions, we were concerned with winning." But, on reflection, Axthelm decided that he was more confused than appalled by Turner's apparent insensitivity to the feeling of relatives and friends of yachtsmen lost in the race. Turner's attitude, he wrote in his column of August 27, is typical of modern-day sports, in which reality has begun to intrude on fantasy and escape. The intense pressure to win, the language of violence, the superhero stars, the modern athlete's "celebrating the good times with almost savage intensity" are, Axthelm wrote, changing the nature of our games and our understanding of them. Nothing brings this out so well as an unexpected tragedy that reminds everybody but the winners that winning is not everything. Perhaps, he suggested, some sports have become popular *because* of their violence.

The theme that ran through Turner's comments about the Fastnet race was that he was in control and unafraid. The only fear he had, he told the American television audience, was fear itself. One of his competitors, Dennis Conner, echoed Turner's pride in fearlessness when he told the *New York Times* that the worst thing about the race was that his boat, *Williwaw,* did not win it. "It's no worse than the Indianapolis 500 race. We'll take our chances. The danger is part of it. We were racing all the time." Read literally, that meant that the Fastnet and the Indianapolis 500 races are equally dangerous, but what Conner probably wanted to say was that, like a race-car driver, he did not fear danger.

Turner and Conner were not alone. Almost every discussion in Plymouth after the eighty-five finishers arrived served as a means of isolating the survivors from fear, just as we in *Toscana* had anesthetized ourselves against our knowledge of the tragedy during our sail in from the Isles of Scilly. Technical information and comparisons provided some security. For instance, just how hard it was blowing in the Western Approaches between 10:00 P.M. Monday and 6:00 P.M. Tuesday was anybody's guess, and, when the ordeal was over and the Plymouth pubs were full, a great many people were engaged in a great deal of guessing. Those who were not in the worst part of the storm and who survived with relatively little difficulty tended to discount the gale's strength in comparisons with storms they had previously experienced. The 1957 Fastnet, the 1977 race between Sydney, Australia, and Hobart, Tasmania, and the 1972 Bermuda Race were prime targets for comparison. Of *Toscana's* crew, for instance, John Coote had sailed in the Australian race and thought it was worse than the Fastnet; Eric Swenson said the 1972 Bermuda Race gale was the toughest storm he had experienced.

Well, then, how hard was it blowing? Fifty-five knots, sixty-five, *seventy*? And the waves—twenty feet, thirty, *fifty*? "Absurd," somebody would say, "it was never near sixty. In the 1957 Fastnet we . . . ." Eventually, the parrying and thrusting would get around to another question, the answer to which might provide some meaning for the calamity. That question was: "How did all those people die?" The only answers that seemed at the time to be emotionally acceptable were, "They made mistakes" or "Their boats broke up." Since there was no evidence either to prove or to disprove these explanations, the unsettling, true answer need never have been confronted. That answer, of course, was: "Because it was a truly terrible storm." To give that answer would be tantamount to admitting that *any-body* could have died in the Western Approaches, and most people prefer not to believe that life is so uncertain.

People had been killed in sailboats, everybody knew that. A bad choice of season, poor seamanship, and unseaworthy boats had taken their share in the *Fleetwing, Hamrah,* and *Airel* tragedies. Those were technical problems, manageable in properly equipped modern boats sailed by the right people. They all could be explained. But what was threatening about the Fastnet tragedy was that *so many* people had died in so many boats. How could anybody grasp that fact without feeling personally affected and that had *somebody* to be at fault?

---

*Siska's* boom broke as the storm began to die, and her crew reefed the mainsail and trimmed it without the spar. *A. M. Patrick*

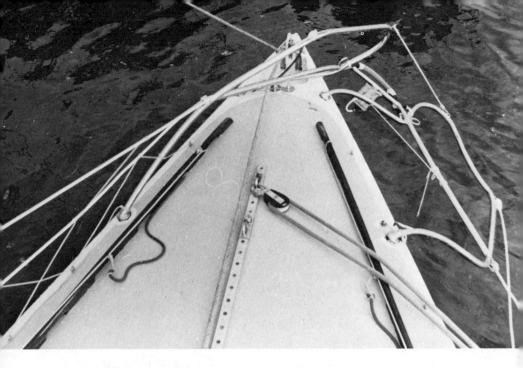

Many boats lost pulpits and lifelines when their masts broke. This is *Jan Pott*'s mangled bow pulpit. *Barry Pickthall*

*At left:* More than a dozen boats lost rudders. *Tiderace*'s rudder exploded and bent in the heavy seas. *Peter Johnson*

*Condor,* one of the largest yachts in the race, set a spinnaker when the wind was still stronger than force 7 and sailed past *Kialoa,* which had been first around Fastnet Rock, to be first to finish. The spinnaker was doused after the spinnaker sheet block broke during a wild broach and cut clean through this stainless-steel stanchion. *Barry Pickthall*

Elsewhere, the argument that modern yachts are not sea-worthy was particularly satisfying to people who owned older boats, who disliked the thought of offshore racing, or whose understanding of boats and the sea was based more on reading C.S. Forester's Hornblower novels or Joshua Slocum's *Sailing Alone Around the World* than on practical experience. When it turned out that only five boats sank and that there was relatively little structural damage, the "bad boat" explanation was quickly jettisoned for another theory: the people who got in trouble had asked for it. They were inexperienced "Sunday sailors" with little knowledge of and even less respect for the traditions of the sea. "Many crews regard the Fastnet as a week's holiday, something to talk about when they get back home," one survivor, Richard Hughes, told the *Daily Mail.* "But when the weather turns like it did, people on board just aren't experienced enough to cope." Presumably, everybody else regarded the Fastnet as a week's work. Conditions that the Sunday sailors found dangerous and terrifying, true seamen experienced as a challenge.

The strongest criticism was reserved for the twenty-four crews who had abandoned their yachts. Since it was commonly believed that any boat afloat was safer than any life raft, the survivors and the press could come up with no explanation for the abandonments other than that the crews had panicked. There simply was no logical reason for leaving one's ship. When most of the abandoned boats that had been reported by their crews as sinking were found afloat, the critics saw further support for their attacks on the seamanship of the abandoning crews. The reports of seven deaths in or near life rafts (from *Gunslinger, Trophy,* and *Ariadne*) further encouraged the critics.

Since the complete stories of most of the boats that were abandoned were not known for weeks or, in, many cases, are told for the first time in this book, many of the criticisms were based solely on a general rule of the sea: don't leave the ship.

**Several boats were rolled so violently that crew members were thrown against steering wheels with enough force to bend the rims. This happened on *Tenacious, Morning Cloud,* and, illustrated here, the United States Naval Academy's *Alliance*. Peter Cook**

Yet the critics chose to ignore available evidence that the life rafts did save many sailors. For every man who died near a life raft, some fifteen were rescued out of one. Several survivors had suffered serious injuries that could never have been properly treated in the wrecked cabin of a wildly rolling yacht. Despite this evidence, it became widely believed that many underexperienced crews, composed of beginner sailors who never belonged in the Fastnet race to begin with, became terrified by a little rough weather and irresponsibly abandoned their structurally sound boats. Other crews, this theory continued, were surviving nicely until they were lured off their boats by Royal Navy helicopter crews. If everybody had stayed in his boat, there would have been only a few deaths.

For those who sought easy answers, who wanted to find some lesson in the calamity, and who themselves survived, this was a wonderfully attractive explanation. Initially, I was inclined to accept this theory because, based on *Toscana*'s experience, I thought that the storm was not exceptional. Granted, I felt somewhat proud of our seamanship, and if we had succeeded in winning the race, the ego inflation which seemed to grip Ted Turner so tightly might have been tempting. Rarely does any man have opportunity to claim that he has beaten the elements. But the Plymouth bar talk quickly became transparent. Story after story from the boats that were distressed soon indicated that we were all trying to inoculate ourselves against the awareness that, at its worst, the storm was much more dangerous than, say, the 1972 Bermuda race gale, and that there had been excellent reason to be frightened.

We were engaged, then, in a kind of siege mentality. We could only admit so much about what really happened out there, like soldiers returning home from the front, afraid to confess that they had been tempted to turn tail and run like their comrades down the line. We would say this about the Western Approaches on August 14: the waves were steep, damn steep, but not steep enough to kill a true sailor; that the wind was strong, but not strong enough to blow over a solid boat; that it was bad all right, but not so bad that it forced able seamen to take to their life rafts like Sunday sailors. And we would not admit to having been frightened by vicious knockdowns, curling breakers, flooded cockpits, swinging booms.

This attitude infuriated loved ones who, having feared for our lives through the confused and frequently inaccurate stories that came out of Plymouth, embraced us tearfully only to hear that we had never been fearful, much less in danger. One skipper whispered to me after the race, "It really was a *great* sail, the best one I've had in years." Only good taste prohibited him from repeating his memory to a public that knew that while he was out enjoying himself in the Western Approaches fifteen people drowned and hundreds more had their wits scared out of them. Whether or not my friend passed on his sentiments to his family and friends, I do not know, but his basic feeling about the race was not too different from mine or, for that matter, from Ted Turner's. When I told my closest friend that I had never been frightened and had felt challenged to my utmost, she said, with considerable heat, "I hung around the telephone for three days with tears in my eyes worrying that you were dead, *and you were out there having a good time?*"

Not until six weeks after the race was I able to recreate the experience and notice, for the first time, that responsibility and almost interminable activity had desensitized me. While a passenger on a small ferry boat heading to Block Island, which is about fifteen miles off the coast of New England, I stood on deck studying the waves. The ferry rolled with a familiar rhythm: swing to starboard, jerk, swing to port, jerk, swing to starboard. Looking forward, I saw miles and miles of waves methodically curling down at me. They were small and did not break, but they were so perservering, so ubiquitous. . . . I went into the cabin and read the newspaper.

One of the few skippers who both finished the race and admitted publicly to fear was Edward Heath, who, with Turner, was one of the two certifiable celebrities in the Fastnet. The

---

OVERLEAF: **Former prime minister Edward Heath's** *Morning Cloud,* **a member of the British Admiral's Cup team, finished the Fastnet race under a greatly demoralized crew after a bad knockdown. Heath is the man leaning against the lifelines near the stern.** *William Payne*

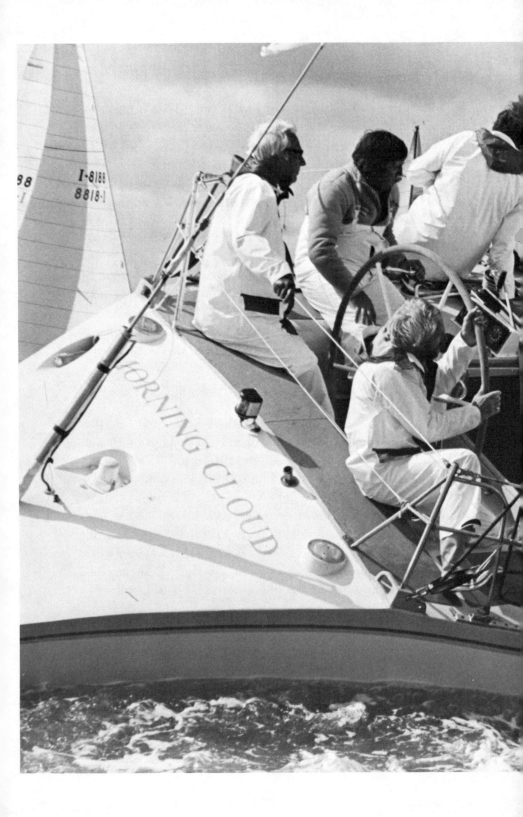

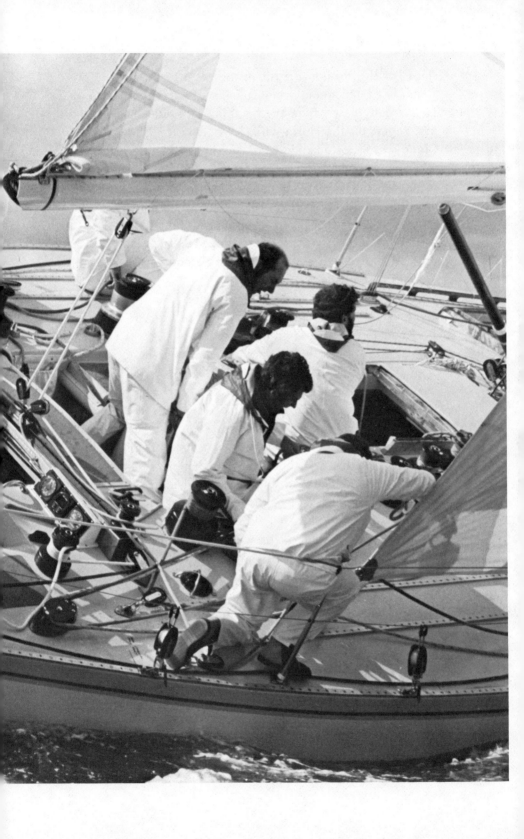

status of the former British prime minister and his *Morning Cloud* had been an important concern of the press. Even *Lloyd's List*, a daily newspaper for the shipping trade, had opened its first report on the storm with, "Mr. Edward Heath's *Morning Cloud* was reported rudderless and in trouble yesterday after a savage storm which was feared to have claimed at least two lives in the Fastnet race." When, to the surprise of *Toscana*'s crew, *Morning Cloud* finished at 5:45 P.M. Wednesday, a hoard of reporters and photographers clomped in their hard-soled shoes and high-heels over the decks of a dozen yachts to the ineffectual protests of a dozen angry crews, and stood waiting to capture Heath's first words.

Normally dapper, composed, and alert, Heath looked drawn and tired. He did not mince words: "It was the worst experience I ever had. We were fighting massive seas. It was very frightening—the sort of thing you would never want to experience again." When a wave knocked the boat over, he told the reporters, he was thrown across the cabin and badly bruised. Two men, he said, were almost washed overboard. The tabloid newspapers the next day ran headlines such as "Ted: My Worst Hours" with photographs of a relieved Heath sipping a beer. A few days later Heath elaborated somewhat on his experience in a column in a Sunday newspaper, although he continued to underplay the seriousness of the near capsize, in which several men actually were thrown overboard, and he did not explain the rumor of rudder damage or why *Morning Cloud* finished so far behind most of the other Admiral's Cup boats (*Toscana* gained four hours on her after Fastnet Rock). Heath never took advantage of his position in the public eye to claim for himself any special powers, skills, or knowledge. His hesitancy fully to dramatize *Morning Cloud*'s misfortunes and his crew's demoralization may have been based on a sincere respect for the agonies of the sailors much more unlucky than he. He may also have been sensitive to the memories of the tragedy of a previous *Morning Cloud* which, in 1974, had sunk in the English Channel after two crew members (one his godson; Heath was not on board) were lost and drowned. A week after the storm, in an article in the *Daily Telegraph,* Heath made constructive criticisms of the Royal Ocean Racing Club's regulations on radios and of the weather forecasting agencies, arguing that two-way radios should be required in all boats and that the time delay between weather forecasts and broadcasts should be reduced by the meteorological office. He also suggested that safety equipment be more thoroughly inspected before races and that authorities develop rules that would encourage stronger boats. Not once did he criticize the seamanship of his competitors.

Once the extent of the disaster became known, the Royal Ocean Racing Club inevitably became the focus of attention. Some people, including the widely respected yachting journalist Jack Knights, criticized the club for not calling off the race when the gale forecasts were made Monday afternoon. Many journalists looked to the RORC and its salaried secretary, Alan Green, for enlightenment on and comment about how such a tragedy could have come about.

In this most introverted of sports, the RORC was unprepared to defend or even to explain itself to the outside world. Before the gale, its officers and officials, many of whom were sailing in the race, had anticipated that their greatest problem would be with the calculation of the final standings. When the storm broke, Alan Green was preparing to settle down for two days in the Plymouth breakwater's lighthouse in order to record the times of finishers and John Clothier, a rear-commodore of the club, was feeling disappointment at having to miss sailing the race in his own yacht, *Polar Bear.*

By Tuesday afternoon, Green, Clothier, and members of the RORC and Plymouth's Royal Western Yacht Club were improvising an emergency procedure in consultation with the military rescue services, compiling a list of the boats that had actually started the race, contacting the next of kin of dead or missing yachtsmen, and trying to cope with a clamoring and confused press. A very high priority was to account for all the entrants via reports from helicopter crews and lifeboats and by requesting yachtsmen to call in their status over marine radio or, if they were ashore, by telephone. Unfortunately, few radio frequen-

ceies and telephone lines were available, and many crews either
did not hear the requests to report that were broadcast over
commercial radio or did not have the ability to transmit messages. Through Wednesday there remained a large number of
boats in a category called "Not Accounted For."

Intended to be noncommittal, this phrase soon became a
synonym for "sunk" in the minds of some reporters and frightened relatives and friends of Fastnet race crews. In England
there were enough backup information services at hand to provide confirmation that a boat in this category was presumed safe,
but in the United States concern for the lives of twelve sailors
took a turn toward pessimism when most of the American boats
were reported as not accounted for. In the confusion, somebody
came to believe that two boats representing the United States in
the Admiral's Cup, *Imp* and *Williwaw*, had sunk and that *Aries*,
the third boat on the team, had probably sunk.

The rumor spread like the plague in the United States
through newspaper offices, boating magazines, and even the national sailing authority, the United States Yacht Racing Union.
Confirmation was almost impossible, since the three boats had
not yet finished and the telephone lines into Plymouth were
jammed. Obituaries of some American sailors were published in
their hometown newspapers. On Wednesday the *New York
Times* inserted the reports of the sinkings into a front-page story
on the race, citing a spokesman for the United States Yacht Racing Union as a source. In every other way accurate and restrained, the *Times* article had been written by Joseph Collins, an
English journalist who worked at the newspaper's large London
bureau. On Thursday, Collins went to Plymouth, from where I
had been telephoning to the *Times* stories about my own experiences and about the rescue efforts. Not knowing about the inser-
tion into his article of the inaccurate news about the sinkings of
the three U.S. boats, he conducted interviews with some American sailors who, when they heard which newspaper he represented, turned coldly polite. Fortunately, Collins did not attend
a press conference at which Alan Green harshly criticized the
*Times* for its "grossly inaccurate" reports. Surprised by the out-

burst, an Australian reporter asked Green how he felt about his country's newspapers. "I'll include Australian newspapers in that charge," Green answered tersely.

One had to sympathize with Green's testiness. A reserved, cautious man who had been hired a year or so earlier to organize races, he obviously was uncomfortable at his daily press conferences when some reporters continued to ask questions along the lines of, "When are you going to stop drowning people?" Suddenly a subject of massive public interest now that it had been unlucky enough to be involved with a major tragedy, ocean racing and its traditions remained distant and complicated in the minds of people used to the immediacy and simplicity of spectator sports such as football.

"Why wasn't the race canceled when you heard the storm warnings?" Green was asked several times. He pursed his lips, looked at the floor, and in measured words said, "The way the sport is organized, it is the skipper's responsibility to decide whether to race or not."

"What should the public think about so many yachtsmen risking their lives and the lives of the men in the rescue services?"

"Public opinion will have to make up its own mind," Green answered. "And sailors must make up *their* own minds whether they wish to face the risks of the sea."

"A Labour MP, Sydney Bidwell, says that the RORC should help pay for the cost of the rescue services because yachtsmen are 'well-heeled, well-to-do people indulging in a fairly expensive sport for their own pleasure.' What do *you* have to say about that?"

For once, Green did not look at the floor while he answered. "I have no comment."

Each press conference included a prolonged line of questioning about weather forecasting: was it timely and sufficient? Green argued that the storm was so fast-moving and violent that it was exceptional—"freak" was a word that he used frequently. Although this appeared to let the meteorological office, which had been taking severe criticism for tardy forecasts, off the hook,

**Alan Green.** *Jonathan Eastland*

the weathermen came back at Green to argue that the storm was by no means freakish. Small intense depressions can form anytime, they said, and, in fact, three times in the twentieth century there had been deeper depressions during August. Neither Green nor the sailors seemed willing to argue such a fine point. Although many people were, like Edward Heath, critical of the lagtime between weather forecasts and weather broadcasts, some critics admitted that even a timely forecast of a force 10 gale would not have given sufficient warning to allow most of the Fastnet fleet to get to port before the worst part of the storm struck.

At each press conference, Green was flanked by survivors who, in one way or another, testified as to the violence of the storm. One was Syd Fischer, an Australian whose *Ragamuffin* was a member of the winning team in the Admiral's Cup. Australia has a reputation for weather of the most violent kind, so when the reporters—none of whom, except myself, had sailed in the race—heard Fischer say that the storm was perhaps as bad as any he had seen at home, they were impressed. Fischer estimated the peak wind speed at seventy knots.

Jonathan Bradbeer, an RORC rear-commodore, described his race in *Eclipse*, the English boat that finished second, as "far and away above anything we've experienced before." It was, he continued, "a great experience" to go so fast under a small jib alone. Frequently, these speakers were introduced by two club officers whose own boats had been unable to finish because of damage—Commodore Donald Parr, owner of *Quailo*, and Rear Commodore John Clothier, who owned but did not sail in *Polar Bear*, whose crew had been rescued by the *Overijssel*.

These points began to sink in by Friday, as the first euphoria of surviving wore off the sailors and most journalists finally came to understand that there was no villain to track down. The removal of the two bodies from the *Overijssel* may have helped to put a perspective on the tragedy; so also might have a memorial

OVERLEAF: **A body is carried from the *Overijssel* after she docked at Plymouth on Thursday, August 16.** *Press Association*

service held at the Plymouth Cathedral after a somber prize awards ceremony. More than two thousand people attended the memorial service, including four Royal Navy helicopter pilots from Culdrose. Some survivors held a fund-raising party at a local pub for the Royal National Life-boat Institution. Reports about the massive and heroic rescue efforts, in fact, did much to elevate people's concerns above petty bickering and self-serving criticisms.

Queen Elizabeth sent this message to the RORC: "I have been following the course of the Fastnet race with much distress. Prince Philip joins me in sending our deepest sympathy to the families of those who died. I have much admired the courage and skill of the rescue teams in their unceasing efforts to rescue the survivors."

It is natural, the *Daily Telegraph* noted in a wise and sensitive editorial, for people to look for scapegoats and to believe that tragedy is avoidable, but "If we still value the qualities of daring, comradeship, and endurance in our national life we should cherish the sports which foster them with the risks they carry. The lessons of Fastnet should be studied calmly and applied sensibly but in the knowledge that they can never expel danger from yachting and the conviction that it will be a sad and bad day when this seafaring people declines the challenge of the ocean."

# 10 Lessons Learned and Unlearned

**T**HE SURVIVORS OF *Grimalkin, Trophy,* and *Ariadne*—
boats that lost nine of the fifteen men who were killed
during the Fastnet race—had immediate concerns
other than talking to the press.

After Nick Ward and the body of Gerry Winks were lifted
from the deck of *Grimalkin,* they were flown to Culdrose, where
doctors ordered Ward transferred to Treliske Hospital, in Truro.
There, he was given medication intravenously, and the doctors
told him that his leg, though badly bruised, was not broken.
Surgeon Commander C. W. Millar, a doctor based at Culdrose,
telephoned Ward's anxious parents with the happy news that
their son had been the 122nd person rescued on Tuesday, August 14.

The last the Wards had heard from *Grimalkin* was a message
relayed on Monday evening by David Sheahan's wife, who reported that all was well in the boat. Having been kept awake
most of Monday night by the strong winds that buffeted their
house in Hamble, near Southampton, the Wards arose to the
first radio reports of death and destruction in the Western
Approaches. Mrs. Ward went to work, leaving her retired husband, Stanley, to worry over the radio. At 12:30 P.M., John
Clothier, the Royal Ocean Racing Club rear-commodore who
had not sailed in the race, telephoned from Plymouth to say that
a life raft containing three survivors of *Grimalkin* had been
found, but that Nick was not aboard. Mr. Ward picked up his
wife from her job and they telephoned the bad news to another
son and their daughter. With their son, Simon, and his wife, the
Wards stood by the telephone and radio much (as Mrs. Ward
later recalled) like wartime families waiting to hear news about

---

*Ariadne* **on Friday, August 17, moments after she was towed into Penzance, Cornwall.**
*Cornish Photonews*

relatives caught in an air raid. They attempted several times to get through to the RORC office in Plymouth, but the lines were engaged. When their daughter, Cheryl, telephoned the club's clubhouse in London, she was told to call Plymouth, but she also encountered busy signals. Meanwhile, Mrs. Ward's brother, who lived in Plymouth, went to the RORC office but there was no news there. The long, agonizing watch over the telephone was finally ended by Surgeon Commander Millar's call at 9:30.

The Wards drove to Plymouth on Wednesday, where they stayed with relatives and talked to Nick over the telephone. The next day they were allowed to pick him up at the hospital. Among his visitors during his recuperation had been the bishop of Truro, a reporter from the *International Herald Tribune,* a representative of the Seaman's Mission asking if Nick needed help in order to return home, Mike Doyle, and Margaret Winks. Nick told Mrs. Winks of her husband's last moments on the heaving deck of the little sloop and of his message to her.

Several days after his release, Nick Ward joined Matthew Sheahan on a trip to Ireland to inspect *Grimalkin*, which a fishing boat had towed into Baltimore. Nick remembers sensing tension between them—something he had also noticed when Mike Doyle visited him in the hospital—yet their common interest in the boat seemed to smooth over any harsh feelings about the abandonment of Ward and Winks by Sheahan, Doyle, and Dave Wheeler. They knew from photographs that somebody had gone aboard and cleared away the mess of tangled rigging, and they also knew that the boat was still floating. When the bus they were riding drove down a hill to the harbor, Ward became excited: there was *Grimalkin*. The driver asked them if they were part of her crew, and they said they were. "Well," he responded genially, "don't tell anybody here or everybody in town will want to buy you a drink." They somehow kept the news of their arrival quiet.

When they went aboard, they found that some money had been taken—possibly by salvagers as reasonable compensation for the rescue—but in most respects she was ready to be rerigged and taken to sea again. Sheahan and Ward set to work cleaning *Grimalkin* up and planning for future races.

Stanley Ward was not willing to forget that his son had been left for dead. Although he respected Nick's desire to forgive the three men who abandoned *Grimalkin*, he made it clear that he thought the decision to leave them was unseamanlike. How strongly his feelings were influenced by his relationship to Nick may be judged from the warm, thankful letters that he wrote to Surgeon Commander Millar and to the parents of Peter Harrison, the young midshipman who had dropped down to the sloop from the Royal Navy helicopter. "It does seem to me," Mr. Ward's letter to the Harrisons ended, "that despite the gloom and tragedy which seems to cover our dear land, there is still bright hope for the future whilst young men like your son, and perhaps our Nicholas, flourish and prosper."

*Trophy*, three of whose crew died after their life raft split apart, drifted in the Western Approaches for two days before HMS *Angelesey*, the Royal Navy fishery protection vessel, took her in tow during the gale that sprang up Thursday. While under tow, the dismasted *Trophy* capsized twice and the *Anglesey* finally let her go on Friday. She was soon taken under tow again by a power yacht on her way from Sweden to Portugal, which pulled her into Falmouth.

Her owner, Alan Bartlett, became an unwilling celebrity of the disaster because he was the brother-in-law of a popular English comedian, Eric Morecomb. After being interviewed by Nicholas Roe for an excellent story about *Trophy*'s experiences that appeared soon after the gale in the *Sunday Telegraph,* Bartlett tired of the attention and stopped talking to writers. Simon Fleming, the ginger-bearded man who had hauled Bartlett out of the water and was later left to drift alone in a section of the raft, shaved off his beard and went back to sailing. During a race the weekend after his ordeal, Fleming discovered two things: first, his arms were so weakened and sore that he was almost helpless in the boat; second, he was frightened, and he several times asked himself if the boat he was in would capsize. He looked forward to sailing in another Fastnet race, but, he has asserted with the same anger that may have kept him alive that cold Tuesday morning, "I'll never get into a liferaft before the boat sinks. I'll lay somebody out before I do that again."

After the *Nanna* rescued him from *Ariadne's* capsized life raft, Matthew Hunt called his mother on the coaster's radio telephone. Mrs. Hunt was nearly frantic when she heard the news of the gale, for not only was her nineteen-year-old son out in the Western Approaches, but also her husband was aboard *Morningtown*, the RORC's escort vessel. Dr. Hunt was no less worried. While *Morningtown* stood by such damaged yachts as *Trophy*, her radio blared out reports of distress, among them the deaths of four men from *Ariadne*. Not until Tuesday night did Dr. Hunt know that Matthew was alive and Mrs. Hunt believe that both her husband and her son were safe.

Matthew himself did not know until Wednesday morning that, as he suspected, Hal Ferris had died. On the front page of the *Daily Mail* was a large photograph of an airman dropping down to a comatose man floating face up in a life jacket, his hands folded across his chest. Ferris was still breathing when he was hauled into the helicopter, but his eyes were rolled back. Despite continuous mouth-to-mouth resuscitation performed by the airmen, he died during the short flight directly to Treliske Hospital. He had survived in the water for over five hours, longer than anyone could have reasonably expected.

First reported sunk, *Ariadne* was recovered and towed to Penzance, where she lay for almost three months under the care of the Receiver of Wrecks. Apparently she was vandalized sometime between her abandonment and her arrival at Penzance, the intruders cutting through the bulkheads that separated the cabin from the cockpit, perhaps to remove electronic instruments that Hal Ferris and his crew had installed so carefully. In early November, she was hauled out of the water, placed on a flatbed truck, and taken to Plymouth to be sold.

Matthew Hunt was a sad young man when he returned to his home near Colchester, in Essex, and the public response to the

An airman drops down to Frank Ferris, the owner of *Ariadne*. More than any other photograph, this one, published in newspapers worldwide, spoke of the horror of the Fastnet race storm. Barely alive when this was taken, Ferris died two hours later in the Truro hospital. *Royal Navy*

race and to *Ariadne*'s tragedy did nothing to cheer him up. Few people knew much about the boat except that her owner had been an American and that she had lost more people than any other yacht in the race. There were nuisance telephone calls and outright criticisms in the press of the crew's seamanship. Matthew and Rob Gilders visited with Bob Robie's widow and sons, who were eager to know what had happened, and they attended David Crisp's funeral. Matthew's strong, supportive family and friends rallied around and tried to cheer him up. His friends were able to convince him to learn the exuberant sport of windsurfing, and he was made happy by the news that he had been accepted into medical school and so could follow in his father's footsteps.

In late August, stung by attacks on Hal Ferris's judgment by Bob Fisher, yachting correspondent of the *Guardian*, Matthew Hunt wrote the following letter, which soon was published in the newspaper:

Sir: I would like to reply to an article by Bob Fisher in which he criticizes people in the Fastnet race for ignoring safety "rules." He made particular reference to the yacht *Ariadne* as an example of a boat whose crew abandoned ship when it was not necessary.

I entirely agree that one should stay with the boat for as long as possible. In my opinion, however, and in the opinion of all the other people on the boat, this is what we did.

On the first roll, we lost the mast, half-filled with water, and a man was badly injured. On the next roll, we lost a man. Had we done a third roll, which was almost inevitable, we might have lost another man or been badly injured by the hard-pointed interior of the boat; we might have sunk without being able to launch the life raft; or we might have lost the life raft—who knows?

Also, having been bailing the boat for a long time, we would probably have been too exhausted to cope with another knockdown.

I also feel it is worth mentioning the terrific feeling of security once we were in the life raft, and I'm sure that the psychological boost gained from this enabled us to keep going for a few minutes longer—very valuable moments in my case.

Matthew Hunt
Colchester, Essex

Although several bodies of men thought to be Fastnet race fatalities were discovered in fishing nets pulled aboard trawlers along the Cornish and Irish coasts, the remains of Bob Robie and Bill LeFevre were not found. Neither was the body of David Sheahan, owner of *Grimalkin*.

Memorial services were held for the Fastnet dead in Sydney, Australia, Cowes, and, in November, the RORC's own service at St. Martin's-in-the-Fields church in London. The lord mayor of Plymouth established a fund for the families of men who had died in the race to which almost £21,000 (over $45,000) eventually was contributed—£12,000 ($26,000) by the Australian government. The Royal National Life-boat Institution directed a special appeal to non-British sailors who had sailed in the race. The British Yachting Journalists' Association awarded its annual Yachtsman of the Year award not to a race winner, as is the custom, but to Alain Catherineau, skipper of *Loreleï*, the French yacht that had saved seven survivors from *Griffin*. Some Americans proposed an award that would honor the memory of those who died in the race by being given to racing sailors who display conspicuous gallantry and seamanship in rescue attempts.

After the general-audience press moved on to other subjects, the autumn issues of British, European, and American yachting magazines were filled with technical studies of the storm itself and of what might possibly have gone wrong, most of them written from a practical, what-can-we-learn-here point of view. Only in the regional news columns of an English magazine, *Yachting Monthly*, was the intensely human side of the tragedy replayed from month to month as local correspondents mourned the deaths of friends, repeated accounts of individual experiences aboard boats that survived the storm, described the heroism of the rescuers, and praised the warm reception provided to distressed yachtsmen by harborside towns—particularly those along the coast of Ireland.

Except in those columns, the flood of descriptions, analyses, and opinions died down in November as everybody awaited the report of an inquiry into the race that was conducted by the Royal Ocean Racing Club and the Royal Yachting Association. Apparently worried about possible government interference in their activities, and obviously desirous of learning as much as possible about the storm and the ways in which crews and boats reacted to it, the inquiry committee devised and mailed to each of the skippers three copies of a questionnaire that asked about the race in enormous detail, with more than 230 questions. The survey was about as thorough as one could hope, although it did take some things for granted. For instance, when it asked the skippers for information about barometer readings, it assumed that all boats carried barometers. Most did; this is the most basic means of evaluating weather. One boat that did not was *Aries*, Michael Swerdlow's forty-six-footer that was a member of the American Admiral's Cup team, whose crew apparently felt that weather broadcasts would tell them all they needed to know. In addition, since the questionnaire would be evaluated by a computer, many of the answers were in a "yes/no" format. There was no provision for "maybe," which sometimes was the only possible answer.

In any case, the inquiry received back completed forms for 235 boats, plus forms for another 30 that were returned too late for evaluation. The final seventy-six-page report released on December 7, less than four months after the gale, was based on the experiences of 78 percent of the boats in the fleet. (Since the questionnaires were to be distributed by each skipper to the two most experienced crew members, a total of 669 actual questionnaires were returned; the committee did not describe how it handled differences of opinion between crew members in the same boat.)

Briefly, the report confirmed that this storm was something special. About 70 percent of the respondents estimated maximum wind speed at force 11 or above (fifty-six or more knots), and the significant (or largest average) wave height at greater than thirty feet (44 percent thought the largest waves were forty feet or more in height). The effects of this seaway were extraordinary. Forty-eight percent of the boats reported knockdowns to horizontal or almost horizontal. Thirty-three percent reported that they had experienced a knockdown beyond horizontal, including a 360-degree roll—a total of seventy-seven boats. (Unfortunately, the question was misleading and it would have been easy to indicate that a rollover had been experienced even if a boat was knocked down to just beyond horizontal. Conservatively assuming that only half of those boats—thirty-eight—were actually rolled over entirely, one-eighth of the entire Fastnet fleet still experienced the catastrophe of a complete capsize.) Of the twenty-three respondents who abandoned their boats, all but one experienced a complete rollover, and while a disproportionate number of smaller boats were rolled entirely over, six of the forty respondents in Class I (boats between about forty-four and fifty-five feet) claimed to have been rolled over.

While there was data to suggest that the lighter, shallower boats such as *Grimalkin*, which have become popular in ocean racing over the past two or three years, may have been more vulnerable to these catastrophic knockdowns than heavier boats such as *Toscana*, the inquiry committee was not able to state absolutely that a causal relationship existed between the type of boat design and ability to take the seas in the Western Approaches. Forty-three percent of those knocked over answered yes to the question, "Would any boat of similar size inevitably have suffered a knockdown?" (the same percentage did not answer and only 13 percent answered no).

Some other data: 14 percent experienced "significant" structural damage, 11 percent suffered damage to steering gear, and 18 percent suffered "significant" damage to the mast. One-third said that entry of water was a problem; 11 percent said that the amount of water in the boat affected the decisions that were made. Serious injuries occurred below in 5 percent of the boats, almost all of them during rollovers. Eleven percent of the respondents experienced at least one instance of safety harness failure. Twelve life rafts were washed overboard, and of the fifteen that were used, five capsized.

The inquiry addressed the questions of crew experience and knowledge by asking how many long-distance races of various lengths the skippers had sailed and then factoring the results against the record of knockdowns and damage. Experience levels were high. Seventy-seven percent of the skippers had sailed in seven races between one hundred and two hundred miles long, 56 percent had sailed in seven or more races between two hundred and five hundred miles long, and 55 percent had sailed in at least three races longer than five hundred miles. A slightly disproportionate number of the less experienced skippers experienced rollovers and hull or rig damage, and a disproportionate number of the most experienced skippers did *not* have problems—but once again, the differences are small.

What was the greatest danger? "Steep breaking sea"—44 percent; "knockdown/capsize"—16 percent; "crew injury," "man overboard," and "rig damage"—6 percent each.

Answers to various questions indicated that all four traditional storm tactics—lying a-hull, running before it with warps dragging and without warps dragging, and heaving-to—worked about equally well. Three-quarters of the respondents said they would use the same tactic again. In the words of the committee, "No magic formula for guaranteeing survival emerges from those who were caught in the storm. There is, however, an inference that active rather than passive tactics were successful and those who were able to maintain some speed and directional control fared best." That certainly was the experience in *Toscana*, *Police Car*, and *Lorelei*, whose skipper found that he could conduct the rescue only when he approached *Griffin*'s life raft at speed. The committee concluded that other factors at play in avoiding bad knockdowns included the skill of the helmsman and whether or not a boat was unlucky enough to be caught by an especially bad wave. While Britain's Institute of Oceanographic Sciences told the inquiry that the Labadie Bank could not have influenced wave height or shape, 57 percent of the respondents to the questionnaire felt that the depth of water affected the sea conditions.

The crews that abandoned their boats believed that the risk of staying on board was unacceptably high, the committee reported, although two boats "were abandoned simply on the grounds that the life raft was likely to provide more security than the virtually undamaged hull of the yacht." (The inquiry committee did not cite by name boats other than the three that rescued competitors.) The committee praised the rescue services and, while pointing out that error is inevitable in such unusual conditions, the seamanship, navigation, and courage of the yachtsmen themselves.

Neither two-way radios nor a smaller fleet nor any other single factor would have forestalled disaster, the committee appeared to conclude. This was an experienced group of sailors exposed to an exceptionally severe sea condition. Some of the boats may not have been quite as stable as they should have been, and some equipment should have been stronger, yet as elucidated in the report's last paragraph, the lesson was: "In the 1979 race the sea showed that it can be a deadly enemy and that those who go to sea for pleasure must do so in full knowledge that they may encounter dangers of the highest order."

Whether drawn from narratives or statistics, this lesson did not at first seem universally understood—or, if it was, it may have led some people into and not away from great risks at sea.

On September 21, five weeks after the storm, thirty-two men and women started a race from Penzance to the Canary Islands, from where they would race to Antigua. Each sailor was alone in a boat no longer than twenty-one feet. Twenty-five boats had finished at Tenerife by late October. Of the others, three sank, two quit the race because of leaks, and two more were not accounted for. Fortunately, nobody died. In the 1977 running of this race, which was called the Mini Transat, two people were lost.

While this race was under way in the autumn of 1979, a Massachusetts real estate investor named John Tuttle was preparing his boat and a crew for a sail across the North Atlantic Ocean. *Desperado,* an extremely lightweight 57-foot sloop, was waiting in New York City for a gale with which she could tag along as it crossed the ocean. Tuttle's goal was to break the record of a bit over twelve days for the fastest transatlantic passage by a sailing vessel, set in 1905 by the 185-foot, three-masted schooner *Atlantic.* When the propitious storm appeared, *Desperado* got under way. On December 8, her mast damaged, and several sailors injured after encounters with two gales, *Desperado* was abandoned in mid-Atlantic by her nine crew members, who were picked up by a British container ship. "When the mast

OVERLEAF: **The Irish yachting port of Crosshaven. Some of the yachts which abandoned the race made fast near the Royal Cork Yacht Club.** *Irish Times*

was jammed into the trough" of a forty-foot wave, Tuttle told the *New York Times,* "we stopped like we had hit a brick wall. Food exploded out of the refrigerator and flew into the navigation station. Cottage cheese became a lethal weapon."

Later that month, during a gale off the coast of Australia, a yacht named *Charleston* went down with five hands while being sailed to the start of the race from Sydney to Hobart, Tasmania. *Charleston* was a new, untested thirty-five-footer. A few weeks after *Smackwater Jack,* a well-tried boat of about the same size, disappeared during a storm while she was returning to New Zealand from the finish of the race. In her four-person crew were her designer, Paul Whiting, and his wife. That same storm forced *Condor of Bermuda,* the huge sloop that had been first to finish the Fastnet race, to lie under bare poles for three days in seas reportedly as high as fifty feet. While nothing more may ever be known about the loss of the nine sailors, surely these victims of the sea—like the fifteen men of *Grimalkin, Trophy, Ariadne,* and the other unlucky yachts in the Fastnet race—had rushed willingly down the hills to the water, only to find themselves caught in the wrong place at the wrong time. Who should judge whether they were there for the wrong reason?

# Acknowledgments

**T**HE HELP AND ENCOURAGEMENT given me while I conducted research for and wrote this book might appear to be the result of an international conspiracy. That I sailed in the Fastnet race is due to Eric Swenson, who asked me to join him in *Toscana*—an American boat named after a region in Italy. Eric eventually became a source of information, a sounding board for ideas, and my American editor.

The idea of writing a book on the gale and the havoc it wrought was first suggested to me by Sir Peter Johnson, an Englishman who, as the seventh baronet of New York, has American blood in his veins. Peter sailed in the race, and served as a research assistant and my English editor.

I conducted research in England during three trips in August, September, and November, 1979—a total of seven weeks in London, Essex, Hampshire, Devon, Cornwall, and the Isles of Scilly. My hostesses, who were unfailingly hospitable and tolerant of my ridiculous schedule, which often included dawn departures and midnight arrivals, were Mrs. Blanche L. Prescott, of Putney Heath, London, and Lady Caroline Johnson, of Lymington, Hampshire. Peter Johnson, his partners, Erroll Bruce and Richard Creagh-Osborne, and the pleasant and efficient staff at Nautical Publishing gave me the freedom of their office and helped me over many logistical hurdles.

I talked with dozens of survivors of the storm, many of whom are named in the text, but I especially would like to thank three men who courageously relived for me their painful experiences in boats that suffered fatalities: Nick Ward, of *Grimalkin;* Simon Fleming, of *Trophy;* and Matthew Hunt, of *Ariadne.* They are three of the bravest men I know. Other veterans of the race who were helpful were John Coote, our navigator in *Toscana;* Gary Jobson, Jim Mattingly, and Greg Shires, of *Tenacious;* John Kilroy, of *Kialoa;* Dave Kilponen and John Marshall, of *Aries;*

Larry Marks, of *Morning Cloud;* Malin Burnham, of *Williwaw;* German Frers, Jr., of *Acadia;* Dave Allen, of *Imp;* and Chris Bouzaid, of *Police Car.* Pat Wells and Peter Webster, who were aboard *Morningtown* and HNLMS *Overijssel,* provided information about the rescue effort. Mrs. Robert Robie and her family very kindly took time at a difficult moment to talk with me about their husband and father, who was lost from *Ariadne.*

Matthew Lethbridge, coxswain of the St. Mary's lifeboat, gave over most of a day to answer my questions about lifeboat duty, the Isles of Scilly, and his crew's service during the Fastnet gale. Brian Jenkins, also of St. Mary's, and Toby West, coxswain of the Falmouth lifeboat, also helped this American understand that most English of organizations, the Royal National Life-boat Institution.

The following provided unpublished reports and letters about or photographs of the storm: Alain Catherineau, of *Lorelei;* John Ellis, of *Kate;* Major J. K. C. Maclean, of *Fluter;* George Tinley, of *Windswept* (whose record was a twenty-page transscript of a telephone conversation with Richard Creagh-Osborne, whom I thank again); Peter Cook, editor of *Yachts and Yachting;* and John Driscoll, then assistant editor of *Yachting World.* Major Hall, editor of *Yacht Racing/Cruising,* and Bill Wallace, of the *New York Times,* arranged for me to cover the Admiral's Cup and the Fastnet race for their publications, thereby providing me with press credentials.

My old friend Eric Olsen appeared in Plymouth at the very moment when I agreed in principle to write this book, and the next day, August 19, he offered me the benefit of his considerable knowledge of boat construction and seamanship during a brainstorming session as we drove along the narrow roads of Cornwall. After we returned to the United States, we spent another fruitful day studying weather maps and tracking the gale, and he later offered several insights into the causes of the calamity in the Western Approaches.

Erroll Bruce, who probably knows more about going to sea in small boats than any other man, read early drafts of the manuscript and was helpful on the subject of the psychological effects of storms on sailors. Ingrid Holford, in Lymington, and David J. Schwab, of the Great Lakes Environmental Research Laboratory at the University of Michigan, provided information about wave formation. Steve Lirakis, of Newport, Rhode Island, provided insights about safety harnesses. Hal Roth and Harvey Loomis gave the final manuscript thorough, helpful readings.

Three public relations offices were helpful. Second Officer Judy Sherwood and Chief Petty Officer Pete Ferris provided photographs, allowed me to interview a helicopter crew, and clarified printed reports during my two visits to the Royal Naval Air Station at Culdrose.

Tim Hunt, press officer at the Southern Rescue Co-ordination Centre at Plymouth, gave me access to his file of clippings and explained the mechanics of the search and rescue services. And the staffs at the London and Poole offices of the Royal National Life-boat Institution supplied information about the lifeboats.

I would like to emphasize that at no time did I receive special assistance from the Royal Ocean Racing Club, which was extremely busy with its own—very different—study of the gale and its effects on the Fastnet race fleet. The report of their inquiry (conducted in partnership with the Royal Yachting Association) was by my side as I was completing the manuscript on December 14, and I have summarized its major findings in chapter 10. Theirs is a thorough analysis based on questionnaires filled out by over two hundred skippers. This book, on the other hand, is a narrative based on interviews and published material about some seventy yachts and rescue craft. We appear to agree on every important conclusion. Sailors interested in highly technical matters will find the report fascinating; it is available from the Royal Ocean Racing Club, 2 St. James's Place, London SW1A 1NN, or from the United States Yacht Racing Union, P.O. Box 209, Newport, Rhode Island 02840.

Finally, I would like to thank several people who have helped during the four months I worked on this book by providing the perspective that every author needs. Charles Taylor and my friends on Roosevelt Island, New York, helped me to understand some personal reactions I have had to the calamity. My parents provided important housekeeping support and were enthusiastic guinea pigs for various drafts of the manuscript. Ann Marie Cunningham, lately of the Presidential Commission on the Accident at Three Mile Island, in her own way encouraged my attempt to understand and explain an event about which she has unpleasant memories, knowing that my work on this tragedy has been as important to me as her work on another disaster was to her. I hope that the dedication page properly thanks my sons, William Pierce and Dana Starr Rousmaniere, for their patience and encouragement.

J.R.

# Appendices / Sources / Index

# Appendix I

## Summary of Finishes, Abandonments, and Sinkings

| CLASS | APPROXIMATE SIZE LIMITS* | STARTERS | FINISHERS | RETIRED | CREW LOST | ABANDONED AND RECOVERED | SUNK |
|-------|--------------------------|----------|-----------|---------|-----------|-------------------------|------|
| O | 55–79 feet | 14 | 13 | 1 | 0 | 0 | 0 |
| I | 44–55 feet | 56 | 36 | 19 | 0 | 1 | 0 |
| II | 39–43 feet | 53 | 23 | 30 | 0 | 0 | 0 |
| III | 34–38 feet | 64 | 6 | 52 | 6 | 4 | 2 |
| IV | 33 feet | 58 | 6 | 44 | 6 | 7 | 1 |
| V | 28–32 feet | 58 | 1 | 48 | 3 | 7 | 2 |
| TOTAL | | 303 | 85 | 194 | 15 | 19 | 5 |

*Boats were assigned to various classes not by their overall length but by their International Offshore Rule ratings, which are determined by a formula involving many speed-producing and speed-inhibiting factors and which are intended to indicate the potential speed of racing boats. When the race is over, the IOR ratings are factored against the boats' elapsed times on the course to calculate corrected times, which are then compared to determine the overall standings. Since some large boats may have relatively low ratings and some small boats may have relatively large ratings, the "approximate size limits" only indicate the size range of the majority of boats in each class. For example, in Class III there were entered several forty-footers and one thirty-footer. The IOR limits for each class are assigned by the Royal Ocean Racing Club at the beginning of each racing season.

# Appendix II

## Rescue Services

*Fixed-wing Aircraft*    Nimrod Mark 1 aircraft based at Kinloss and St. Mawgan flew a total of 109.25 hours on August 14, 15, and 16. The Royal Air Force Nimrod is an antisubmarine warfare, four-engine aircraft that is also used for search and rescue. It has a crew of twelve and carries eight life rafts for dropping. Its communications include double sideband, single sideband, aero very high frequency and ultra high frequency, and marine very high frequency radios. It is also equipped to receive signals from emergency location transmitters. Closing down two of its Rolls-Royce Spey 250 jet engines, it can fly for extended periods of time, and with facilities for two navigators, it often is designated as on-scene commander in search missions. The first Nimrod assumed this role early on the morning of August 14 before handing over to HMS *Broadsword*.

In addition, one French Atlantique flew for eight hours on August 16, and an Irish Beech King aircraft flew six sorties for a total of 18.3 hours. The total fixed-wing air time was 135.55 hours.

*Helicopters*    Taking off at Culdrose, Royal Navy helicopters flew sixty-two sorties for a total of 195.05 hours. These were Wessex, Sea King, and Lynx helicopters. Flying from Chivenor and Brawdy, RAF Whirlwind and Sea King helicopters flew nine sorties for 17.1 hours. Irish helicopters flew two sorties for 4.2 hours. The total hours for all helicopters were 216.35.

On August 14, helicopters recovered seventy-four survivors and two bodies from yachts and life rafts. On August 17, another body was recovered.

*Military Surface Vessels*    The Dutch frigate HNLMS *Overijssel* and the British fishery protection vessel HMS *Anglesey* participated in the search and rescue operation from the onset of the storm, late on the night of August 13, until August 16. The British frigate HMS *Broadsword* assumed the role of on-scene commander at 5:30 P.M. August 14 and served through August 16. Two tugs, RMAS *Rollicker* and *Robust*, participated in the operation from August 14 through August 16. Other military vessels in the search were HMS *Scylla*, RFA *Olna*, and the Irish patrol vessel *Diedre*.

*Nonmilitary Vessels (other than lifeboats)*   Commercial vessels known to have aided in the search and rescue were MV *Nanna* (the West German coaster that saved the survivors of *Ariadne*), the MV *Chestree*, the trawlers *Sanyann*, *Petit Poisson*, and *Massingy*, and a Dutch trawler carrying a side number "6."

*Lifeboats*   Thirteen Royal National Life-boat Institution stations in Ireland and England were called into service, the first at 10:15 P.M. August 13 and the last at 4:14 A.M. August 16. They served a total of 169.6 hours and towed in nine yachts, escorted in nine yachts, and took a doctor to a yacht.

*Communications*   Unlike the American Coast Guard, in Britain HM Coastguard is a shore-based organization responsible for coordinating rescue services. The Land's End Coastguard station monitors marine radio frequencies and is responsible for much of the eastern Atlantic. The Southern Rescue Co-ordination Centre, at Plymouth, kept in constant touch with the Land's End station and coordinated navy and air force operations.

**Some Rescue Positions**

# Appendix III

Search and rescue helicopters reported the following incidents at estimated positions on August 14. The key numbers refer to the chart above, and the time given is Greenwich Mean Time, one hour earlier than British Summer Time, which is used in the text. Though the yachts in the race were stretched along the course between Land's End and Fastnet Rock, most helicopter activity was evidently in an area centered seventy miles west-north-west of Land's End, and with about a forty-mile diameter.

| KEY NUMBER | YACHT NAME | TIME GMT | POSITION LAT./LONG. N | W | EVENT |
|---|---|---|---|---|---|
| 1 | Magic | 0132 | 50-30 | 7-00 | Rudderless and shipping water |
| 2 | Mulligatawny | 0615 | 50-50 | 7-30 | Dismasted, report of distress |
| 3 | | 0318 | 50-40 | 8-10 | Men sighted in a life raft |
| 4 | Tarantula | 0518 | 50-30 | 7-10 | "Sinking" |
| 5 | Morningtown | 0543 | 50-50 | 7-10 | Morningtown reports sighting red flares |
| 6 | | 0615 | 51-00 | 7-10 | A Nimrod sees red flares |
| 7 | | 0746 | 50-50 | 6-50 | 3 survivors sighted from Wessex |
| 8 | Grimalkin Trophy | 0939 | 49-00 | 7-30 | Grimalkin (3) plus Trophy (2) survivors picked up |
| 9 | Ariadne | 1037 | 50-54 | 7-25 | Frank Ferris (Ariadne) picked up, "in a bad way" |
| 10 | Skidbladner | 1155 | 50-46 | 6-42 | 5 survivors airlifted off |
| 11 | Gan | c. 1200 | 50-41 | 7-38 | 6 survivors airlifted off |
| 12 | Hestrul | c. 1200 | 50-43 | 7-35 | 6 survivors airlifted off |
| 13 | Gringo | c. 1400 | 50-56 | 7-30 | 7 survivors airlifted off |
| 14 | Golden Apple | c. 1600 | 50-16 | 7-18 | 10 survivors airlifted off |
| 15 | Gunslinger | c. 1600 | 50-23 | 7-22 | 7 picked up |
| 16 | Flashlight | c. 1630 | 50-20 | 7-10 | 4 airlifted off |
| 17 | Allamanda | 1755 | 50-30 | 7-30 | 5 crew picked up |
| 18 | Billy Bones | 1755 | 50-40 | 7-30 | 6 crew picked up |
| 19 | Flashlight | 1957 | 50-22 | 6-56 | Found adrift and abandoned |
| 20 | Golden Apple | 1957 | 50-19 | 7-15 | Found abandoned |

# Sources

### Books and Articles

Ames, Ben, "To Cuxhaven in *Hamburg*," "Yachting," October 1936

Axthelm, Pete, "Tragedy in Toyland," *Newsweek*, August 27, 1979

Beck, Horace, *Folklore & the Sea* (Middletown, Ct.: Wesleyan University Press and Mystic Seaport, 1973)

Belloc, Hilaire, *On Sailing the Sea* (London: Rupert Hart-Davis, 1951)

Briggs, Katherine M., *A Dictionary of British Folk-Tales in the English Language*, part B, vol. 2 (London: Routledge, 1970)

Campbell, Joseph, *The Mythic Image* (Princeton, N.J.: Princeton University Press, 1974)

Coles, K. Adlard, *Heavy Weather Sailing* (Clinton Corners, N.Y.: John de Graff, revised edition, 1975)

Collins, Wilkie, "To the Scilly Islands," in *Rambles Beyond Railways, or Notes in Cornwall Taken A-Foot* (London: Westaway Books, 1948)

Elder, Michael, *For Those in Peril: The Story of the Life-Boat Service* (London: John Murray, 1963)

Fowles, John, *Shipwreck* (London: Jonathan Cape, 1974)

Gill, Crispin, *The Isles of Scilly* (Newton Abbot: David & Charles, 1975)

Holford, Ingrid, *British Weather Disasters* (Newton Abbot: David & Charles, 1976)

Holford, Ingrid, *The Yachtsman's Weather Guide* (London: Ward Lock, 1979)

Larn, Richard, *Cornish Shipwrecks*, volume 3, *The Isles of Scilly* (New York: Taplinger, 1971)

Loomis, Alfred F., *Ocean Racing, 1866–1935* (New York: Morrow, 1936)

Luard, W.B., *Where the Tides Meet* (London: Nicholson & Watson, 1948)

Middleton, E.W., *Lifeboats of the World* (New York: Arco, 1978)

Parker, Selwyn, "Anatomy of a Disaster," *Magill*, September 1979

Partridge, Eric, *Origins: A Short Etymological Dictionary of Modern English* (New York: Macmillan, 1958)

Phillips-Birt, Douglas, *British Ocean Racing* (London: Adlard Coles, 1960)

Plym, Gustav, *Yacht and Sea* (London: Adlard Coles, 1961)

Royal Navy, *The West Coasts of England and Wales Pilot,* 10th and
    11th editions
Royal Ocean Racing Club and Royal Yachting Association, *1979 Fast-
    net Race Inquiry Report* (London, 1979)
Van Dorn, William G., *Oceanography and Seamanship* (New York:
    Dodd, Mead, 1974)

The events that occurred in the Western Approaches on August 13,
14, 15, and 16 received immense international attention, and the accounts published at that time in many newspapers and magazines were
important sources. The British and American yachting magazines
listed below published many accounts and analyses of the storm in
issues between October 1979 and March 1980. Nicholas Roe's article,
"Last Race of the Yacht *Trophy,*" in the August 19 *Sunday Telegraph,*
was perhaps the best piece of journalism published immediately after
the race. Another London Sunday newspaper, the *Observer,* devoted
much of its magazine of November 25 to an article about the race,
"Pitch-Poled in the Fastnet," which was one of the few analyses of the
disaster written for the general reader.

### Newspapers

LONDON—*Daily Express, Daily Mail, Daily Mirror, Daily Star,
Daily Telegraph, Guardian, Lloyd's List, Observer, Sunday Telegraph.*
(Due to a strike, the *Times* was not published at the time of the storm.)

PLYMOUTH—*Western Evening Herald, Western Morning News.*

OTHER BRITISH—Camberly *Star,* Falmouth *Packet,* Isle of Wight
*County Press,* Windsor *Advertiser.*

UNITED STATES—*Boston Globe, New York Times, Washington
Post.*

AUSTRALIA—*Australasian Express, Sydney Morning Herald.*

### Magazines

BRITAIN—Devonport *News, Navy News,* Royal Naval Sailing Association *Journal, The Lifeboat, Seahorse, Yachting Monthly, Yachting
World, Yachts and Yachting.*

UNITED STATES—*Latitude 38, Motor Boating & Sailing, Sail, Sea,
Sports Illustrated, The Telltale Compass, Yachting.*

CANADA—*Pacific Yachting.*

# Index